TONY BUZAN

AGE-PROOF YOUR BRAIN

Sharpen Your
Memory in 7 Days

HarperThorsons
An Imprint of HarperCollins*Publishers*
77–85 Fulham Palace Road,
Hammersmith, London W6 8JB

The website address is: www.thorsonselement.com

and *HarperThorsons* are trademarks of
HarperCollins*Publishers* Ltd

First published by HarperThorsons 2007

10 9 8 7 6 5 4 3 2 1

Mind Map® and Buzan™ are registered trademarks
of The Buzan Organization

Tony Buzan asserts the moral right to be
identified as the author of this work

A catalogue record of this book is
available from the British Library

ISBN-13 978-0-00-723310-6
ISBN-10 0-00-723310-8

Printed and bound in Great Britain by
Clays Ltd, St Ives plc

This book is proudly printed on paper which contains wood
from well-managed forests, certified in accordance with
the rules of the Forest Stewardship Council.
For more information about FSC,
please visit www.fsc-uk.org

Mixed Sources
Product group from well-managed
forests and other controlled sources
www.fsc.org Cert no. SW-COC-1806
© 1996 Forest Stewardship Council
FSC

Contents

Acknowledgements

With special thanks to my wonderful support team at HarperCollins: Carole Tonkinson, Publisher; Susanna Abbott, Editorial Director, who also helped me write this book; Jacqui Caulton, Design Manager; Monica Green, Production Director; Liz Dawson, Publicity Manager; and Belinda Budge, Managing Director and Publisher.

A big thank you also to: John Farndon for helping me write this book; Lizzie Hutchins for her superb edit; and Caroline Shott, my incredible Literary Manager, whose energy and dedication constantly amaze me.

Finally, a special thank you to my home team: Anne Reynolds for her tireless and efficient support; my brother, Professor Barry Buzan, for his decades-long belief in me and the Mind Mapping concept; and to my mother, Jean Buzan, who has always encouraged me to pursue my vision for Mind Maps.

Introduction

Be the master of your memory

Stop thinking that every passing year brings you closer to excruciating 'senior moments' and a membership to your local CRAFT club (Can't Remember a Flaming Thing)! It's a complete misconception that your brain automatically deteriorates with age, and there is science to prove it. What is true is that you need to look after your brain, like any other part of your body, in order for it to keep performing well for you, just as your body will struggle to keep up with the demands you place on it if you consistently ignore its welfare. This is what this book is about. Keep your brain fit and agile and it will keep performing as well as you want it to. You will, in effect, be able to age-proof it indefinitely.

Let's take a look at how sharp your mental powers are right now. Your personal assessment is in two parts: the first part is a subjective analysis, the second a series of practical exercises.

How fit is your brain?

PART ONE Where do you think you are?

This subjective analysis is an extremely useful pointer to how mentally agile you are right now. Keep a note of your scores as you will repeat this questionnaire later in the book to help you monitor your progress.

On a scale of 1 (easy) to 5 (real problem), how easy do you find it to remember these things?

Remembering names

- [ ] Someone you've just met
- [ ] Friends
- [ ] Family members
- [ ] Places such as restaurants you've visited
- [ ] Titles of books and movies you've seen

Remembering numbers

- [ ] PIN number
- [ ] Bank account number
- [ ] Familiar phone numbers
- [ ] New phone numbers
- [ ] Doing simple sums

Remembering dates

- [ ] Birthdays and anniversaries
- [ ] Appointments
- [ ] Household chores

Remembering where

- [ ] Where you put things (keys, remote controls, etc)
- [ ] Where you parked the car
- [ ] Directions

Remembering stories

- [ ] What you watched on TV last night, read in the papers, etc
- [ ] What you were just saying
- [ ] What the other person was just saying
- [ ] The right word for it

Add up your scores, and then see how you did:

20–30 Congratulations! You have no memory problems whatsoever. Have fun with the programme and mental challenges in this book to keep your brain in tip-top condition.

31–40 You experience mild memory problems. Follow the programme in this book to fine-tune your brain and try and eradicate them altogether.

41–60 You have average memory problems. Stick with the programme and you will start to excel.

61–80 You have moderate difficulties with your memory and need to follow closely the programme in this book to get your brain back into shape. You should start to notice improvements within 7 days.

81–100 You experience severe memory problems. You can start to improve your performance by using the memory techniques in this book and following the programme. Persevere and you will soon improve your score.

PART TWO The 7-Minute Mind Makeover

This part of your personal assessment is designed to challenge your mental performance in six different areas:

1. **Short-term memory**
2. **Long-term memory**
3. **Language**
4. **Logic**
5. **Analysis**
6. **Creativity**

In fact, doing this 7-Minute Mind Makeover now will already put you on the route to boosting your brain fitness. This is because it will stimulate the flow of blood to your brain and start encouraging it to build new connections, both of which are essential for keeping your brain in shape.

All you need is seven minutes of your time, paper, a pen or pencil and something to time yourself accurately with (most mobile phones have a built-in stopwatch). Follow the instructions carefully – make sure you give yourself only the amount of time specified for each question – then check your answers to see how well you did. (Any answers that you need to look up will be at the back of the book.)

MEMORY TONER

Time: 60 seconds
Focus: Short-term memory

Number punching

Below are series of numbers. The challenge is to remember as many as you can in just 60 seconds.

Cover up the numbers, leaving just the top number of the left column exposed. Memorize it, cover it up and write it down. (Use your writing hand to cover the number to avoid the temptation of simply writing what you see.) Now reveal the second number. Remember it, cover it up and write it down. Go down through the list for 60 seconds, getting as far as you can.

At the end of the 60 seconds, check your answers. How many did you get right? Give yourself one point for each group of numbers you remembered correctly.

4567	34197824
6788	521980935
56899	768956431
12546	1768518945
178498	6548921237
986734	57234568125
7898239	86735159371
7234512	462729138746
89352627	193426987365

SCORE /18

MEMORY BUILDER

Time: 60 seconds
Focus: Long-term memory

Fact bank

Here is a list of the Seven Deadly Sins. Give yourself 20 seconds to remember them. Cover up the book, then write down all the sins you can remember. Give yourself one point for each sin you remember and a bonus point if you remember them all.

Pride	Envy
Lust	Sloth
Anger	Greed
Gluttony	

SCORE: /8

Here are the nine traditionally named planets of the solar system, in order. This time, give yourself 40 seconds to remember them. Cover up the book and write down the planets in the correct order. Give yourself a $\frac{1}{2}$ point for each planet you remember and $5\frac{1}{2}$ points if you remember them all in the correct order.

Mercury	Saturn
Venus	Uranus
Earth	Neptune
Mars	Pluto
Jupiter	

SCORE: /10

WORD POWER

Time: 60 seconds
Focus: Language

Anagram

With anagrams, you swap the letters of one word around to find another. Give yourself 60 seconds to solve these fruity anagrams. The last letters should spell out the name of something they all have in common. Give yourself 2 points for each anagram you solve and 2 bonus points for the extra name.

RICTUS   PAGER

TROPICA   LUMP

SCORE: /10

LOGIC BOOSTER

Time: 60 seconds
Focus: Logic skills

Age-old logic

This time, exercise your powers of logic to work out the ages of these three friends. Allow yourself 60 seconds only. Give yourself 2 points per age correctly answered and 2 bonus points if you get all three.

> George, Tony and John's ages add up to 48
> In six years' time, John will be twice Tony's age
> George's age and Tony's age together equal John's age.
> **SCORE:** /8

ANALYTIC POWER

Time: 60 seconds
Focus: Logic skills

Codebreaker

Can you spot the hidden message in this text message, apparently on a business matter, from a cheating husband to his personal assistant? Give yourself 6 points if you correctly decipher the message.

> Tell Oliver Now If General Happy Triple Yesterday's Orders Under Rating Scheme, Don't Accept Realtor's Loan If Not Guaranteed.
> **SCORE:** /6

CREATIVE THINKING

Time: 120 seconds
Focus: Logic skills

Making connections

Give yourself 120 seconds to brainstorm as many different uses for a penknife as you can by linking the penknife to the following list of words. Be as imaginative and ridiculous as you like!

chair	rain
Saint George	ear
Planet Earth	radio
dinner	spaceship
basketball	butter
wood	France
elephant	bride
clouds	carpenter
bear	kitchen sink
bread	newspaper
shoe	light bulb

Score yourself according to how many uses you came up with:

0–10 uses	2 points
11–20 uses	4 points
21–30 uses	6 points
31–40 uses	8 points
40+ uses	10 points
SCORE: /10	

Add up your scores, and then see how you did:

60–70 Fabulous! You really are sharp as a tack! Keep exercising that fabulous brain of yours with the programme in this book.

45–59 Your brain is pretty fit overall. It is important to keep pushing yourself with the mind workouts in this book. Take note of the areas you scored less well in and make sure you concentrate on these exercises of the programme.

30–44 This is an average score, which, of course, leaves plenty of room for improvement. Make sure you get on to the techniques and programme in this book as soon as possible, as they will dramatically improve your performance.

15–29 Keep reading and get on to the programme as soon as possible. They will get your brain into shape and enable you to access untapped genius within. Stick with the programme and you will be surprised at how quickly you can turn around your mental fitness.

0–14 Don't be disheartened by your score as the techniques and programme in this book are designed to help you turn around your mental performance. The trick is to challenge your brain regularly to get it back into shape and if you persevere you will.

It's not your age that counts

The assumption with tests like these is that the younger you are, the better your score is likely to be. In fact, your score is far more influenced by how fit your brain is. Anybody at any age can be guilty of neglecting his or her mental fitness.

Until quite recently scientists told us that the brain declines with age. In fact there has never been much real evidence for this. For a long while, IQ tests seemed to show that younger people did better than older people, giving rise to the global assumption that intelligence declined with age. It turned out that this wasn't so for two reasons. The first was that it was simply a matter of training: younger people had had more practice doing the kinds of mental tasks set in IQ tests than older people. As soon as older people were trained in these kinds of thinking, their performance levels shot up. The second reason was that the tests were initially done against the clock. If the time pressure was removed, the older people did just as well as their younger counterparts – and it can quite reasonably be argued that older people are slower simply because their experience means they have to sift through more possibilities to reach the answer. Age widens your mental horizons!

Now, using techniques such as fMRI (functional Magnetic Resonance Imaging) scans, scientists have discovered that your brain is a flexible living organism with an amazing capacity for change and development

The nuns of Mankato

The nuns of the School Sisters of Notre Dame in a remote part of Mankato in Minnesota have attracted quite a lot of interest from researchers into brain-ageing – and no wonder. Many of the nuns are over 90 and quite a few well over 100. Sister Marcella Zachman, who featured in *LIFE* magazine, was teaching until she was 97. Sister Mary Esther Boor was working on the front desk until she decided to retire – at the age of 99! Moreover, the nuns seem to suffer far fewer – and milder – cases of dementia and other brain diseases than average.

Professor David Snowdon of the University of Kentucky believes there is a good reason for this. The nuns take the admonition that 'an idle mind is the devil's plaything' very seriously and go to extraordinary lengths to keep their minds occupied. All the time they compete in quizzes, solve puzzles, hold vigorous debates, write in their journals, run seminars and much more. Snowdon has examined the brains of over 100 nuns of Mankato, donated when they died, and he believes that intellectual stimulation makes the brain connectors that normally atrophy with age branch out and make new links.

throughout your life. It is said to be 'plastic' – that is, it can go on programming and reprogramming itself almost limitlessly. It is evidence like this that is convincing scientists that, just like your body, your brain needs exercise to stay fit.

Your brain in your hands, your brain in your thoughts!

The most powerful and important discovery of all is that your brain's performance is under your control to a much greater extent than scientists ever realized before. It has become clear that the future of your brain is primarily in your own hands, or rather, your own thoughts! The extent to which you keep challenging your brain and maintain your thirst for learning has the greatest influence on how well your brain will keep on performing for you.

Age-proof Your Brain combines theory and practice into a training programme that will help you to make the most of your amazing brain, whatever your age. You will learn about different aspects of brain fitness, from mental agility and memory to physical exercise and diet.

The more you know about your brain and how it works, the more you will be able to make use of its remarkable abilities. Even better, the very act of learning about your brain and thinking about how it works is a stimulus as valuable to your brain as good food is to your body. As you read you will also find a whole range of techniques and tips to help you with your brain-training programme and kick start you into action.

The programme itself is divided into sessions of varying intensity and duration. It begins with The 7-Day Get Sharp Plan, which will take up just one hour of your time for seven days. At the end of the seven days you should be noticeably sharper and more mentally agile.

The second part of the programme requires you to set aside time one day a week for seven weeks – The 7-Week Stay Sharp Plan. At the end of this part of the programme you should be feeling as mentally slick as you were 10 years ago – if not more so.

The final part of the programme is about maintaining and building on the progress you have made. There are a few 7-Minute Mind Boosting plans to keep you on track and plenty of suggestions to make sure that your brain continues to perform for you at the highest level. By the time you reach the end of the programme you should find that your mental abilities are developing beyond anything you ever achieved before. Even better, because your brain is working so well for you, you should also find that you improve your quality of life overall – you should be happier, more confident, more adventurous and have renewed your lust for life.

So what are you waiting for? Turn the page to get started!

PART ONE

Chapter 1

Get more from your brain

Whatever you can do, or dream you can, begin it.
Boldness has genius, power and magic in it. Begin it now.
Attributed to Johann von Goethe

Are you ready to begin a programme which will show
you how to boost your brain power, improve your memory and realize your dreams? Your brain is the most powerful tool at your disposal – faster and more complex
than even the largest super-computers. It is quite simply
one of the most amazing things in the universe. Every
day it does astounding things for you – and it can do
more. Learning how it works will help you to use it properly. That way you can get even more from it – and from
your life.

If you could see inside your head, you would see an
astonishingly complex landscape of folds and valleys. This
delicate pink world – which is actually 72–82 per cent
water – allows you to think, love, eat, sleep, wake up, go

to work, run, jump, play sport, watch TV – everything, in fact, that makes you human.

It is a world that is made up of a complex network of minute cells, each a tiny parcel of biochemicals. There are trillions of these cells, including vast numbers of glial cells, which are the brain's 'housekeeping' cells, the cells that help keep it all together. Just 10 per cent of these cells are the real thinking cells – the branching threadlike neurons. All the same, there are over 100 billion of these neurons. What's more, every single one of them spreads its tendrils through the brain to connect with up to 100,000 other neurons. There are more than 100 trillion different ways in which your neurons can connect – that's more than the number of atoms in the entire universe! Moreover, each connection can link up at 10 different levels, meaning there are actually 1,000 trillion possibilities. It is these myriad connections that process every sensation you receive from the world, think your every thought and guide your every action.

BRAIN CELLS

Neurons, the cells that make up your brain, are tiny, as they have to be for so many to fit inside your head. Under the microscope, they look like minute plants with roots at both ends. Out of the bulb, or nerve body, branch hundreds of radiant threads, called dendrites. These are the cell's antennae and they are responsible for picking up signals from neighbouring cells. The long stem is called the axon, and this is the part of the cell that passes on signals to others.

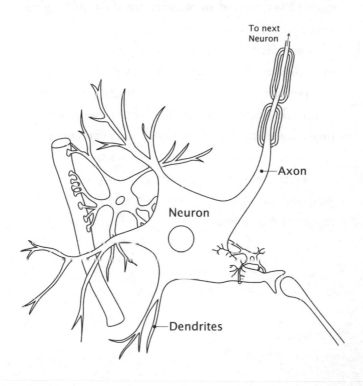

To next
Neuron

Axon

Neuron

Dendrites

Signals are constantly buzzing around your brain – and yet no two neurons ever actually touch. Instead, there is a small gap between them called a synapse. When a nerve impulse is passed on from one neuron to the next, it is carried across the gap by special chemicals called neurotransmitters. There are at least 53 different known kinds of these neurotransmitters. Droplets of them are stored inside the nerve endings in tiny sacs called vesicles. When a nerve signal arrives at the nerve ending, the vesicles drift towards the synapse and spill their contents into the gap. Then neurotransmitters flood across the gap and wash up against neighbouring nerve cells.

Neurotransmitters work in a lock-and-key fashion. For a nerve signal to pass on its message, the neurotransmitter must be the right chemical to fit or unlock receptor sites on the other neuron. If the neurotransmitter fits, it changes the chemistry of the receiving nerve's membrane. This starts off electrical changes in the neuron cell wall, sparking electrical changes that pass a signal along the length of the neuron.

YOUR PLASTIC BRAIN

Not so long ago, scientists were convinced that neurons and their connections were fixed at birth. The idea was that as we went through life, learning new things and gathering new experiences, we simply used up more and more of these connections. Since it was also thought that brain cells died off by the million every day, it seemed inevitable that as we got older, our brains would simply run out of enough space to work well.

Now, thanks to remarkable imaging technology such as fMRI and a raft of ingenious clinical research, this picture has been fundamentally changed. We now know that, amazingly, throughout our lives, our brain connections are constantly changing. All the time, some connections are getting stronger while others are getting weaker. New connections form by the second, while others fall out of use and others are rerouted. Indeed, your brain's neural network is never the same from one moment to the next. Even when you are deep in undreaming sleep, your brain is continually awash with neural activity. Whenever you undergo an intense emotion or are consumed by a complex mental activity, your whole brain seems to light up as countless neurons fire simultaneously. Waves of new activity, each firing its own characteristic pattern of neurons, surge across your brain all the time as external stimuli come in. No neurons fire in exactly the same pattern each time – no experience is ever identical – your brain is changing constantly.

NETWORKS IN THE BRAIN

Whenever a new sensation comes into your brain, it sends a flurry of activity surging through a particular tangle or network of neurons. Each neuron involved both passes on its message to other neurons and sends a signal back to the neurons that alerted it. This feedback loop might amplify the signal, or damp it down.

After the initial signal has died down, the neurons involved reinforce their connections with one another. They are primed and ready to fire again in the same pattern. If the same sensation comes in again, your neurons are ready to fire again that much more readily, like a well-trodden path through the brain. If the sensation is not repeated, the connections begin to weaken, as the path falls out of use. Therefore, the more a particular sensation or action is repeated, the more a particular pattern of neurons is strengthened.

Famously, Michael Merzenich of the University of California, San Francisco conducted some experiments with squirrel monkeys. He put banana pellets in containers just outside their cages and made computer images of their brain activity as they used their fingers to get the pellets through the bars. As the monkeys learned to get the pellets, he made the containers smaller to make the task harder. As the monkeys became more skilled, the area of their brains involved as they used their fingers increased. Once the monkeys completely mastered the task, the area involved shrank again. When the skill became automatic, it was relegated further down the chain of command.

REMAPPING THE BRAIN

Once it was thought that certain areas of the brain were set aside for particular tasks. Medical scientists used to draw wonderful diagrams of the body and brain showing which areas of the sensory cortex – an area around the top of the brain like a headphone band – had nerve endings from different parts of the body. The belief was that these were hard-wired into the brain for life. Now we know that this is not nearly as fixed as scientists once thought. Research conducted by the scientist Edward Taub has shown this to be true. In 1991 he severed the nerves in the hands of some of his experimental monkeys. Under pressure from animal rights activists, Taub abandoned his experiments. Some years later, when scientists examined the monkeys, they found the areas of the brain that once received signals from the now useless fingers received them from the face instead. This proved that the brain can completely rewire itself and that areas not used regularly can be taken over by other functions.

Research also revealed more of the brain's amazing 'plasticity'. Until the mid-1960s, it was thought adults could not form new synapses – connections between neurons. Neuroscientists believed that once brain development ceased after childhood, the synapses were frozen in position for a lifetime. Then research showed that new synapses could actually form after all, again and again. Scientists called this ability to change 'synaptic plasticity'.

The late Christopher Reeve is an inspirational example of how the brain can completely rewire itself and form new synapses. A horrific horse-riding accident in 1995 left him completely paralysed and unable to breathe unaided. For five years his physical condition deteriorated rather than improved. Then in 2000 he started to make some remarkable progress. With the help of Dr John McDonald, a neurological surgeon at Washington University in St Louis, Missouri, Christopher Reeve started to retrain his body and mind. Together they embarked on an intensive programme of therapy whereby different parts of his body were exercised by passing electrical currents through them. Whilst a particular part of his body was exercised, Christopher Reeve used visualization techniques to try to retrain his mind to send the right signals to move that body part.

By November 2000, Christopher had regained control of the muscles of his right index finger. Other fingers followed until he was able to lift his right hand off the table by bending his wrist and to move his arms and legs whilst lying down. By the time he died in 2004 – from an adverse reaction to antibiotics – he was regularly off the respirator, could propel himself through water and feel the touch of a finger on his skin over about half of his body. He was also the first documented paralysis patient who went from state 'A' (total paralysis) to state 'C' (state 'E' is classified as normal).

A MAP OF THE BRAIN

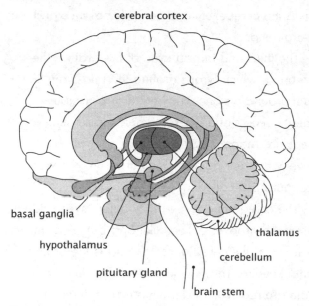

cerebral cortex

basal ganglia

hypothalamus

pituitary gland

thalamus

cerebellum

brain stem

The structure of your brain is complex and varied, and different parts perform different functions.

The most obvious feature is that the brain is in two halves, or hemispheres, known as the left and right hemispheres. These are separated by a deep groove. A huge bundle of nerves, called the corpus callosum, bridges the gap and keeps the two halves in touch.

There are three main regions on each side of the brain. Deep in the middle of each side, connected to the nerves in the spine, is the root of the brain, the brain stem. The brain stem is responsible for basic subconscious body functions such as breathing and heart rate.

Just behind the mid-brain, the top part of the brain stem, is a lump about the size of an apricot. This is the cerebellum and controls balance and co-ordination.

The third and largest area of the brain is the cerebrum, which wraps around the mid-brain like a plum around a stone. It is here that conscious thought occurs and where complex tasks such as speaking, reading and conscious control of movement are triggered. The cerebrum is divided into four parts called lobes.

The cerebrum has a wrinkly outer layer, folded with deep grooves called sulci and bulges called gyri. This is the cerebral cortex and is the brain's control centre. This is where messages from your brain are received and monitored, and where commands go out to the rest of your body.

If you slice the hemispheres apart, you find a complex collection of chambers and tubes of various sizes under the cortex. At the heart of this, just below the corpus callosum, is a ram's-horn shaped cluster called the limbic system. Even though the limbic system is part of the unconscious brain, it has a deep affect on our way of looking at the world, for this is where emotions are generated, and our basic urges and desires arise. It includes the seahorse-shaped hippocampus, which is crucial in laying down long-term memories, and the amygdala, which is where we know when we are scared.

THE AGELESS BRAIN?

The plasticity of the brain has very interesting implications for ageing. We now know that our brains are plastic throughout life. Could we use this plasticity to keep our minds sharp, continually bringing into play new parts of the brain to make up for any deficiencies? In other words, is it possible to age-proof our brains by making changes – whatever our age?

This really does seem likely. What's more, it seems quite plausible that this is entirely *within our control*. We can make these changes *simply by the way we use our brains*.

Taub and his co-workers have already found strong evidence that the brain can be healed by its own plasticity. Amazingly, some people who have lost the use of an arm through a stroke have been trained to use it again by having the good arm restrained and being forced to use the apparently dead one, a technique called 'constraint-induced (CI) movement therapy'. Even though the part of the brain that controlled the arm was damaged, the CI movement therapy forced the brain to open up new areas in order to move the dead limb. Similar results have been produced with speech impairment and even dyslexia. Although this research is still in its early days, Mezernich believes the brain's plasticity may really enable us to protect ourselves against age decline.

MENTAL PADDING

Research from another angle backs up Mezernich's theory about how we can protect our brains from declining over time. Scientists had long been puzzled by the observation that people who led intellectually stimulating lives and were better educated seemed to be better protected against mental decline in old age than other people – even against Alzheimer's disease. In fact, they seemed to be better protected against head injuries, getting drunk and even Parkinson's disease, as well as age. Some scientists said this was just common sense – the more you've got, the more you can afford to lose. Recent research is showing that this mental padding, called 'cognitive reserve', is something more substantial.

What the research shows is that while the cognitive reserve does not actually protect against physical deterioration in the brain, it does seem to cushion people against the *effects* of any damage. For instance, some mental decline in old age is linked to damage to white matter – the part of the brain made by the tendrils that connect neurons. In 2001, research by Laurence Whalley of Aberdeen University found that better-educated people seemed to lose far less of their mental capacity for the same loss of white matter. Two years later, researchers in California showed that highly educated people were less likely to show a dip in

IQ after a head injury. There is a growing consensus that better-educated, more intelligent people are better able to make the most of the brain.

One way this works is through finding alternative pathways. In cases where brighter people have suffered damage to the brain, the brain has been more successful in finding back-up networks to compensate for the loss.

Another way brighter people may do better is by using their brains more efficiently. Yaakov Stern of New York's Columbia University scanned brains of young and old people for mental activity levels and found that the brains of those with high IQs worked much less hard when doing a complex task than those with low IQs. Stern believes that having more efficient networks protects people with high IQs from some of the problems of brain-ageing.

NEW BRAIN CELLS

As if this weren't enough good news, a third line of research is also backing up the growing evidence that mental decline in old age is very far from inevitable. First, research showed that nerve cells could regenerate after injury. Secondly, it showed that new nerve cells were being created in certain parts of the brain, such as the hippocampus, throughout life. Neurogenesis, as this process of creating new nerve cells came to be called, was pretty limited. Still, the fact that it went on at all was a complete surprise – and created a tremendous stir among neuro-scientists. What if it could be stimulated to the level where damage to brain cells could be repaired?

Some researchers are investigating ways to stimulate neurogenesis through new drugs. Others are currently exploring the possibility of boosting neurogenesis with stem cells, the special cells from which new body cells grow. These stem-cell researchers hold out the possibility of reversing age-related brain diseases such as Alzheimer's, Parkinson's and Huntington's.

LEARNING

One of the most astonishing things about the human brain is its remarkable capacity for learning throughout life. A few basic skills are there right from the start, like knowing how to breathe and control your heartbeat and body temperature. Apart from these innate skills, pretty much everything else has to be learned by the brain, and it learns by rewiring connections in response to conditions in the world outside. Give your brain an input and its neuronal wiring will change and learn. Without an input, that wiring stays unchanged, or even withers.

When you're young, your brain has to do a great deal of learning. As a child, your brain is constantly a-buzz with learning activity, and demands twice as much glu-cose energy as an adult's just to keep this process going.

BRAIN FACTS

Neurons that fire together, wire together

Your brain starts to develop from the moment sperm penetrates egg, and it develops at a literally mind-boggling rate. Every second of your mother's early pregnancy, your brain is growing 4,000 new primitive brain cells. Every hour, it is growing 15 million! As they grow, they migrate through the brain to their allocated places – though no one knows how they know where to go. Some never make it.

When they finally reach their destination, the neurons stretch out their connectors to neighbouring neurons. Some make countless connections and thrive; others are isolated and shrivel. Those that do survive are those that are stimulated and make connections with other cells.

This process underlies a key aspect of brain life – *neurons that are used thrive, those that aren't don't.*

Throughout infancy and early childhood, neurons are in constant competition. There are areas of the brain allocated for particular skills such as speech or musical ability. The development of these areas depends on how much they are stimulated and which networks of neurons survive. Although we may inherit certain abilities, this is only part of the story. It is down to nurture to determine which aspects of this natural potential come to fruition. Our entire environment controls the input to our brain – which neurons are stimulated and which are not.

Research on animals has shown that neurons that are stimulated by learning form more and stronger connections with other neurons. More blood vessels grow in areas of the brain that are stimulated, increasing the flow of blood, bringing extra glucose energy and oxygen fuel for the cells. Glial cells, the brain's housekeeper cells, grow apace in areas that are stimulated. The same applies to the process of myelinization, the wrapping of the neuron's transmitting tail or axon in a sheath of insulating myelin, which increases the strength of the neuron's signals. Learning may even stimulate the growth of entirely new nerve cells in the appropriate area.

USING IT

Almost nothing in the brain is set in place. Although neuroscientists can draw maps for regions of the brain controlling different functions – speech, spatial skills and so on – these maps are subtly different for everyone. Competition between neurons means the boundaries are constantly shifting according to the inputs they get.

When parts of the body are frequently used, for instance, the area of the brain devoted to them grows. Scans of the brains of violin players show that they have a much larger area of the brain devoted to the thumb and fingers of the left hand, the hand used to grip the violin neck and finger the strings. The younger the violinist started to play, the bigger this area of the brain is. The more you stimulate areas of the brain with inputs, the bigger and stronger they grow.

One secret of age-proofing your brain, then, is to try something new. You would be in good company. To help keep his approach to scientific problems fresh, Einstein played the violin. To give him a different perspective on politics, Winston Churchill painted landscapes.

BRAIN FACTS

The Mozart effect

Back in the 1990s, American psychologist Frances Rauscher made the extraordinary discovery that listening to Mozart's music improved people's spatial skills and mathematical reasoning. The effect was so marked it could even be demonstrated in laboratory rats negotiating mazes. Soon, Rauscher discovered that a Mozart piano sonata actually activated genes involved in nerve signalling in her lab rats.

In another study, young children given music lessons improved their IQ scores markedly over contemporaries given drama or computer lessons. The same could be true for adults.

MAKING IT AUTOMATIC

The great thing about learning is that the more you do, the easier it becomes. Eventually, some skills become so well learned that your conscious brain doesn't need to think about doing them at all. Driving a car, for example, is a tremendously complex task requiring a huge amount of co-ordination. Yet most drivers are quite able to do this effectively on autopilot, guided by their unconscious brain, while their conscious brain talks about the weather or listens to traffic reports.

Similarly, once you've learned to ride a bike, play the piano, swim, drive or cook a meal, the ability stays with you for life. It may get a little rusty if not used for some time, yet it never goes. Yet all these complex skills take up very little brain power. In other words, learning something well needs less brain power, not more; it makes your brain more efficient.

MIRROR NEURONS: NATURAL MIND-READING

In 1996, three neuroscientists probing the brains of macaque monkeys found that, in addition to firing when the monkeys moved, the brain cells in the area responsible for certain movements fired when they saw another monkey making the same movement. These neurons seemed to 'mirror' the behaviour of another animal. Since then, scientists have discovered that many animals, including humans, have these 'mirror neurons'.

Many scientists believe that these are the neurons that allow us to put ourselves in someone else's shoes mentally, to empathize and understand feelings from another's point of view. Spectators at a football game get deeply involved in the game because their mirror neurons act out all the movements of the players, kicking the ball and seeing it into the goal. Audiences at the theatre go through the emotions of the characters on stage as their mirror neurons fire in sympathy. Italian neuroscientist Vittorio Gallese says, 'We share with others not only the way they normally act or subjectively experience emotions and sensations but also the neural circuits enabling those actions, emotions and sensations; the mirror neuron systems.'

Scientists are now beginning to think that mirror neurons are deeply involved in the way we learn about the world. We collect a whole range of information from the world and then act it out in our heads to build up a picture which enables us to interact with each other effectively.

Although the research is still in its early days, it seems likely that one of the best ways you can learn new skills and boost your mental performance is by making the most of your mirror neurons. When you're trying to learn a new skill, for instance, watch an expert at work very carefully. Watch every movement and try to imagine in your head how you would make exactly the same movements. What would it feel like? Going over this again and again in your head, refining it until you are sure you have it just right, could help you make huge strides with physical practice.

There are many other ways in which you could develop your mirror neurons besides learning new skills. It's essentially about developing your imagination. Whenever you get the chance, concentrate on imagining what it feels like to be someone else. Put yourself in his or her shoes. Think about how that person feels and why he or she behaves in such a way. This helps you develop sympathy and understanding for others and also helps your own brain development.

EFFICIENCY AND WISDOM

Knowledge comes, but wisdom lingers.

Alfred, Lord Tennyson

Another way of looking at this might be in terms of wisdom. You could say that wisdom is the ability to grasp the essence of complex situations and act accordingly. It makes complete sense that it is associated with old age. This ability to spot the important things can come only through a long process of trial, error and success (see page 184). By the time we are older, we have been exposed to countless situations, and each one has provided our brain with input. We have learned from both our successes and our failures.

Also, recent studies have shown that the older we get, the more stable we become emotionally. Our brains become much less prey to neuroticism and negative emotions, helping us to see things clearly. Of course, older people could have told you this long ago. Now, though, there is increasing scientific evidence to back it up.

Scientists are also beginning to realize that with the right brain-training you can boost your IQ. IQ is closely connected to your working memory, the amount of current data you can store in your head at any one time. Torkel Klingberg at the Karolinska Institute in Sweden is a cognitive neuroscientist researching the development and plasticity of the brain during childhood, in particular the development of attention and working memory. With the help of a specially devised training programme, he has demonstrated that the neural systems used in working memory may actually grow in response to training. What's more, the children who completed his training course did better in tests conducted as part of the experiment *and* found their scores in IQ tests leap by 8 per cent.

The implication is that with the right kind of training, you can make yourself more intelligent. This is an appealing idea in its own right and may help age-proof your brain. This is what the training programme in this book is all about.

BRAIN FACTS

Becoming an expert

Some people astonish us with feats of expertise –
the memory champion who remembers great
strings of numbers, the pianist who can sight read a
difficult score while talking to his class of singers,
the computer analyst who can hack his way into the
nation's defence network.

With the aid of modern scanners and research
techniques, scientists have begun to study the
brains of these amazing experts and they have
discovered that they are no different from anyone
else's. In fact, it is highly likely that most of us can
become an expert in any field we want. All we
need is the motivation to learn the skill. That means
putting in the time and effort, of course. Dedicated
practice lays more and more information down in
your automatic memory – the memory that takes up
no space in your working memory and allows you
to do things without even thinking about them. With
practice, estimates suggest it takes about ten years
to become what most people acknowledge as an
expert, and the rewards are great.

AGE-PROOFING YOUR BRAIN

Your brain is amazing – and it can stay that way. As we've seen, science is confirming now what a lot of people have been saying for some time – that brain function does not have to decline with age. If you use your brain in the right way and keep challenging it, you can develop its astounding potential at any age. This book shows you how. Its tips and techniques will help you to make the most of your brain right now and to build on this in the future. With the help of this brain-training programme, you can make the most of your brain, including its incredible memory. Let's take a look at how your memory works – and then at how you can improve it.

Chapter 2

Your memory has no limits

The true art of memory is the art of attention.

Samuel Johnson

For most of us, one of the biggest worries about getting older is losing our memories. Indeed, memory loss has become so associated with 'old age' that Grandma having a 'senior moment' is the stuff of TV sitcoms. Yet your memory has no limits – whatever your age. Many older people may take a little more time to remember things, yet once the memory is there it seems as good as at any age.

Rather than expect to have more and more episodes of forgetfulness as we grow older, we should remember just what can be achieved. There are plenty of examples of great mental longevity. Michelangelo's greatest works date from his sixties and he was still creating masterly work when he died at the age of 89. Goethe completed his famous *Faust* at the age of 82, just nine months before his death. In more modern times Vera Stravinsky was a professional painter whose personal philosophy was, 'You work in this life.' She painted every day up until the day she died at 97 and remained as sharp as a tack to the end. Dr Paul Sherwood is a practising 90-year-old Harley Street doctor in London. He still works five days a week, as he firmly believes you have to stay engaged to stay alive.

My own mother, Jean Buzan, is 90 years old and another inspiring example of what you can achieve if you stay active and interested throughout your life. She is certain that if you believe in yourself and continue to stimulate your brain, 'You're not getting older, you're getting better!'

This can definitely be true of your memory, and the techniques suggested in the next chapter show just what you can do to improve your recall – at any age. Let's begin by asking …

WHAT IS MEMORY?

Memory is many different things. It's that recollection of the day you spent on the beach in the rain as a child. It's your ability to write a letter without thinking how to hold the pen and shape the letters. It's what enables you to hold in mind the beginning of this sentence even as you read the end … In fact, memory is involved in everything you ever learn or experience. Memories are being made, stored and remembered every single moment of your life.

When you remember something, your brain does it by creating a new series of pathways of nerve connections, called a 'memory trace'. When you forget, it is because the connections break down through lack of use. Memory is a complex, multi-layered task that draws in every part of your brain. Some memories are restricted to particular parts of the brain; most draw in scores of interacting networks, or even the whole brain at once. Even those that end up in a particular location often link up to many different areas.

Originally, psychologists thought they would find that each memory had its own location in the brain. If they had the right tools, they thought, they could, one day, identify the group of neurons, or even the single neuron where a memory was stored. Although there are indeed parts of the brain associated with particular skills, we now know that the site association of even these skills is far from rigid. Indeed, it seems likely that most memories stimulate the entire brain.

What's more, most memories are very far from being unchanging records. Each time a memory is used, it changes slightly. When you go out for a meal, for example, your frontal cortex, the logical part of your brain, will organize the physical details of the event into one kind of memory. Your amygdala, your emotional centre, will add an emotional meaning to these memories. If you remember feeling very good that night, the memories get attached to a good feeling. The following week, you find your dinner partner has gone off with another person. When you now try to recall the dinner, it has a very different emotional context. The memory gets a different tag and you remember it in a very different way. The interconnections involved in the memory trace have shifted.

HOW YOUR BRAIN STORES MEMORIES

Although research is still at an early stage, some psychologists think even the simplest of memories are stored in groups or networks of neurons in many different parts of the brain, rather than one single location. They may even be stored in the nervous system beyond the brain. When you remember something, the elements are reassembled at what neurologist Antonio Damasio calls 'convergence zones' located near the network of sensory neurons that first registered the event.

There is growing evidence to suggest that the hippocampus – in the middle of your brain and in touch with both hemispheres – sends out new memories to the brain and reassembles them when needed. Interestingly, it seems to do most of its memory storage when you're asleep. In the same way that a computer backs up data automatically in the night, your hippocampus seems to despatch the memories of the day for storage when you're asleep and dreaming – which may be why a good night's sleep is so essential for learning.

It's neurons, ultimately, that store memories, and they do so by firing and making connections with other neurons. Each memory is a particular firing pattern of neurons – not a single neuron. It's a network. As we have seen, each new experience strengthens some connections and weakens others. After the experience is over, these changes would quickly fade away if it weren't for a phenomenon called long-term potentiation, or LTP, in which links between particular groups of networks are strengthened. LTP means the more an experience is repeated, the stronger these networks become, making the memory stronger.

BRAIN FACTS

Think young, stay young

In China, older people are still generally revered for their wisdom and 'old age' does not have the same negative connotations that it does in the West. Interestingly, in a Harvard study researchers compared the memory performance of a group from China with one from the USA. They found no difference in performance between young people from each group. However, the older Americans were outperformed by the older Chinese, who had a much more positive attitude to ageing. Similarly, Americans who had a positive outlook on age performed better than Americans who had a negative outlook.

The lesson is clear: if you expect your memory to fade and your mental powers to decline as you get older, then your expectations may well come true. If you expect to enter later life full of wisdom and with stronger mental powers than ever, it is far more likely that this will be the case.

How the brain creates lasting memories

Memories are basically groups of neurons that fire together in the same pattern. Whenever the connections are reactivated, they bind together into single memories by LTP. When, say, neuron 1 is fired, it will set off its neighbouring neuron. This brings receptors in neuron 2 to the surface at the connection between the two neurons, making it readier to fire in future. Neuron 2 stays in this standby state for days, needing only a weak signal from neuron 1 to set it off. If that signal comes, it will become even more primed and the bond between them will become so strong that they will always fire together. When they do so strongly, their combined effect is so powerful that they may trigger a neighbouring cell. If this happens repeatedly, this third cell too is drawn into the group, forming a lasting memory.

Types of memory

SENSORY MEMORY

The briefest form of memory is your sensory memory. This is the memory that briefly holds the input from all your senses. At any one time there is so much incoming information that the sensory memory retains it just long enough for your brain to sort out what's useful and discard the rest. This is what enables you to go on seeing, hearing and feeling something momentarily after it stops. You can write your name in the air with a sparkler at night, for example, because, if you are quick enough, you will be able to see the last letter while your eyes are still holding the sensory memory of the first. This visual sense memory is called your 'iconic memory'.

If you've ever had the experience of thinking you haven't heard something, then remembering you have just as you are about to ask for it to be repeated, that's your sound or 'echoic' sensory memory at work giving you the playback.

SHORT-TERM AND LONG-TERM MEMORY

Your memory can work in the short or long term. Your short-term memory is when your brain stores things for a few seconds, minutes or maybe at most hours. This is what you use when you look up a telephone number in your address book and remember it just long enough to key it in on your phone. It's actually essential for day-to-day functioning and so many psychologists prefer to call it 'working memory'.

It is your short-term memory that enables you to hold the beginning of a sentence in your head as you listen to the rest. It also acts as a filter, storing only information that seems to be important and shutting out all the otherwise overwhelming bits of data that are streaming in through your senses all the time.

In some ways, working memory is a little like the RAM on a computer. Although it holds just enough data to perform tasks, the data vanishes as soon as the computer is switched off. For this kind of memory, the neurons can manage quite well with the proteins already there in the synapses. To store a memory long term, however, the neurons have to make new proteins. Recent research suggests that the creation of these proteins is triggered by a protein called CREB. This very special protein also seems to be involved in a number of long-term changes to the operation of the brain, such as the adjustments to your body clock after jet lag.

EXPLICIT AND IMPLICIT MEMORY

Once a memory is stored for the long term, you don't necessarily remember it consciously. Some memories are 'explicit', which means you can access them – or at least try to! These include factual knowledge such as names, places and dates. These memories depend on an interchange between the hippocampus and the front of the brain – the temporal lobe. Memories like this are made quite quickly, recalled quickly or forgotten – like a gigantic, instant access library that is also rather changeable.

Some memories, however, simply bed down slowly to become part of the brain's programming. These are the 'implicit' memories that exert their influence without you being aware of them. All the skills and habits you learn through life are like this – walking, talking, eating, picking up a cup, kicking a ball and so much more. These memories of procedures, or 'procedural memories', as psychologists call them, take time to acquire. You have to go on practising them again and again until they are established. Once you've got them, you rarely have to think about them again.

MEMORY MAESTROS

Throughout history there have been a number of great memorizers whose reputed feats are astonishing. The ancient Greek Themistocles knew the names of 20,000 citizens of Athens. He was a slouch compared with Seneca, however, who is said to have known the names of *all* the citizens of ancient Rome.

In the seventeenth century, the famous Italian scholar and bibliophile Antonio Magliabechi was given charge of the 40,000 volumes in the library of the Grand Duke of Tuscany in Florence. It is said he memorized every single word of every single volume! His memory for words was so prodigious that the story goes that an author once decided to test him by giving him a manuscript to read very quickly. After Magliabechi returned the manuscript, the author pretended that he had lost it and asked Magliabechi to help him remember what he could. To his amazement, Magliabechi wrote down the entire book without missing a single word or punctuation mark.

Some people are able to use phenomenal working memories to do amazing mental calculations. In the nineteenth century Johann Zacharias multiplied two 20-digit numbers in his head in just six minutes. In 1980 a remarkable Indian woman, Shakuntala Devi, is believed to have multiplied together two 13-digit numbers in just 28 seconds. Just try this on paper with half that number yourself and you'll begin to see what an astonishing feat this is:

745629 x 456231

The Holy Grail for mind sport champions today is memorizing pi, 22 divided by 7, to as many decimal places as possible. When the Indian Rajan Mahadevan did this to 31,811 decimal places in 1985, it seemed the bar had been set unbeatably high. Then the Japanese got interested. In 1987, Hideaki Tomoyori worked out pi to 40,000 places. In 1995, Hiroyuki Goto worked it out to 42,195 places. And in 2005, Akira Haraguchi apparently did it to an astonishing 83,431 places!

EPISODIC MEMORY

Psychologists sometimes divide conscious, explicit memories into episodic and semantic. Episodic memories are your multimedia memories. They are memories of entire episodes in your life in all their aspects – the day you learned to skate, your first day at school, your evening out last Sunday, with sights, sounds, smells, conversation, the lot. You can often remember all the aspects of the episode almost as if you were reliving them. Memories like these seem to draw in connections from all over the brain.

Most episodic memories fade over time, and require more and more effort to recall in detail. Often the memory changes – coloured by all kinds of influences, including fear and stress – and we remember things differently at different stages of our lives. The most intense experiences are burned almost indelibly in our minds, while everyday occurrences soon fade.

FLASHBULB MEMORY

Particularly powerful episodes seem to fire up the entire brain like a flashbulb. They make neurons fire so intensely all over the brain that even little details are remembered. Most of these 'flashbulb memories' are personal memories of emotional moments, such as your first day at school or your first kiss. Some are common to many of us, such as a team or nation winning a sporting event.

SEMANTIC MEMORY

Semantic memories are our memories of individual snippets of information – facts, opinions and objects. Knowing Paris is the capital of France is a semantic memory. Your day trip to Paris is an episodic memory. Yet it may be you remember that Paris is the French capital *because of* your day trip to the city. Semantic and episodic memory can be interwoven.

Interestingly, though, a recent study of London children suffering long-term amnesia from damage to the hippocampus revealed a striking difference. Neuropsychologist Faraneh Vargha-Khadem found that while the hippocampus damage deprived them of episodic memories, their semantic memory was intact. Although they could read and write well and had as good a head for facts and figures as any of their classmates, they couldn't remember a TV programme they'd just watched.

It seems likely then that the hippocampus's role is to firm up the connections between memory traces left in different parts of the brain. This is why the vulnerability of the hippocampus may be crucial as we get older.

The flexibility of memory

The brain's memory store has revealed itself to be far more flexible than anyone ever imagined. John Ratey cites the example of a brilliant young American violinist called Martha Curtis. As she grew up, Martha suffered such disturbing epileptic seizures that doctors decided they had to remove the part of her brain responsible for her seizures. The problem was that the part involved was that identified with musical skill. Surgeons cut away a little at first, fearing Martha would lose her musical gift. Eventually they had to remove the whole area in order to stop the seizures. Remarkably, the surgery, though stopping her fits, had no effect on her musicianship at all – she played as beautifully as ever. It turned out that when she had learned the violin as a child, her brain had simply rewired itself and sent the memories of her skill to another, undamaged region of the brain.

This flexibility is just one example of the amazing power of the brain. The next chapter looks at how you can tap into this and use it to improve your own memory – whatever your age!

Chapter 3

Quick-win memory techniques

The mastery of some simple mnemonic system may lead some people to realize, for the first time, that they can control and modify their own mental processes.

Hans Eysenck

How good do you think your memory is? Do you think it could be better? Just how good do you think it can be? Some people can perform astonishing feats of memory. There is a famous story about Mozart visiting Rome in 1770, when he was 14, and listening to Allegri's *Miserere* in the Sistine Chapel. This beautiful half-hour long piece was considered so special that the Vatican forbade its publication. After the concert, Mozart wrote down the entire thing from memory. More recently, memory champions have been setting world records which seem nothing short of miraculous to ordinary people. Can you imagine, for instance, memorizing the order of every single playing card in a pack? Dominic O'Brien can do it in just 32.9

seconds. What's more, in 2003, at the age of 44, he memorized the order of the cards in 18 packs – all 936 cards – in just 60 minutes.

Such feats seem so astounding that it is easy to assume that the people who perform them must have very special brains or be amazingly clever. In 2002, scientists decided to put this to the test and performed a range of tests on highly ranked memorizers at the World Memory Championships held annually. The tests were exhaustive, yet revealed that the memory champions' brains were no different from anybody else's. Moreover, they performed no better in intelligence tests than 'normal' people. What the researchers did discover, though, was that nine out of ten of the memory champs were simply using a technique that dates back to the time of Ancient Greece, called the Method of Loci, which is based on location and imagination (see page 78).

What's more, other tests of memory champions have shown that they are very good at tasks to which they can apply similar techniques. At every other memory test they are no better than anyone else. A good memory is simply a skill, and a skill that can be learned – at any age.

However good your memory is now and whatever age you are, you can improve your memory substantially by using the techniques outlined in this chapter. These powerful quick-win strategies for success will boost your mental agility almost immediately, as they work with your brain, not against it. The 7-Day Get Sharp plan in the next chapter will help you practise them until they become second nature. To begin with, spend some time getting to know the various techniques in this chapter and finding out which work best for you. You will be amazed!

How to improve your memory

What many of these techniques have in common is that they work by linking the thing to be remembered to some other idea. Your brain remembers things best if they have meaning. An event or fact that has a special meaning to you is encoded far more powerfully than one that has none. When a memory has meaning, your brain gives it a tag that makes it that much easier to retrieve.

In the absence of special meaning, a similar memorability is achieved when you see something in context, or linked to some other idea, which provides a tag or hook for the memory. This tag is especially effective if it is lively and surprising – and so memorable – in itself. This seems self-evident. If you imagine your memories as a library, it's clearly that much easier to find a particular memory if it has a big bright colourful tag attached to it.

You'll be amazed by how dramatically you can improve your ability to remember things if you use this combination of association, vibrancy and imagination. You'll find an immediate dividend as soon as you start developing your memory skills. And the more you use them, the better you'll get. Practise these simple methods and you'll find that in just a few weeks, you'll be astonishing yourself by how well you remember things.

Eventually, the ideas should become second nature – you'll apply them without even realizing you're doing it. And, as with all skills, you'll get better with time!

MIND MAPS

The first technique I'm going to show you is one that will help you remember anything you want when you want – and to generate new ideas, organize your life and a whole lot of other things too.

Mind Maps® are a thinking strategy and note-taking system that I invented some 30 years ago and which are now used by many millions of people around the world. Mind Maps are used by governments, educational authorities, schools, multinational corporations and leading businesses and have helped people to:

1. **come up with brilliant ideas**
2. **get a clear grasp of complex topics**
3. **set goals and achieve them**
4. **motivate themselves and others**
5. **improve memory**

They are actually the simplest quick-win memory technique to learn and can have an immediate impact on your memory, creativity and ability to concentrate.

This brilliantly simple idea works because it mirrors the way your brain works and brings together your wide range of thinking skills. When you write down ideas conventionally, you write them down in a list, one after another. Your brain doesn't work like this at all. It fires off signals in all directions, making connections all over the place. Mind Maps make the most of this. They free the mind by helping make thinking fun.

The idea is to start by drawing a simple image of your topic in the centre of a blank page, and to then allow your ideas to spread out in all directions across the page like routes out from a city-centre map. Say you want to plan your week ahead. How do you do it?

1. Gather all the materials you need – your research, an array of coloured pens and a large blank sheet of paper.
2. Turn your paper sideways to let your ideas expand in all directions.
3. Draw a simple image or symbol to represent your central idea – in this case you could draw a calendar.

4. In the case of your week ahead, start by thinking of the various things you have to do. You might have a family party or a swimming lesson and a meeting at work. You could arrange your thoughts by what you will be doing each day.

5. As you think about each main topic of your Mind Map, add a main branch to the central image and write a key word or draw a simple image on the branch. Here you could add a main branch for each of the days of the week. Each word or image must have its own branch.

6. Now explore your main branches with sub-branches. Add single words or simple images to each sub-branch. On Monday, for example, you might have a meeting so you can add details of who it is with, when it is and where.

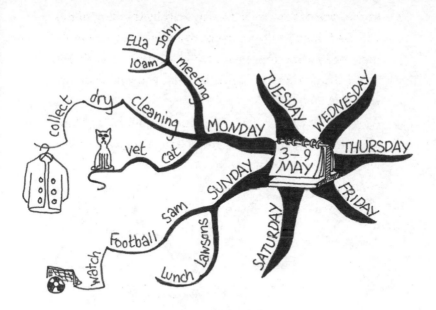

Mind Map tips:

1. Use at least three different coloured pens to make your map vibrant and exciting.
2. Draw curved lines rather than straight ones, because your brain finds them more exciting.
3. Use single words and images at each point.
4. Feel free to come up with ideas anywhere on the map. Don't try to work around in a systematic fashion.
5. Work quickly and freely, without stopping to question your ideas at each turn. Enjoy the process. Make it a brainstorm, not a brain drizzle.

Here are just some of the ways you can use Mind Maps:

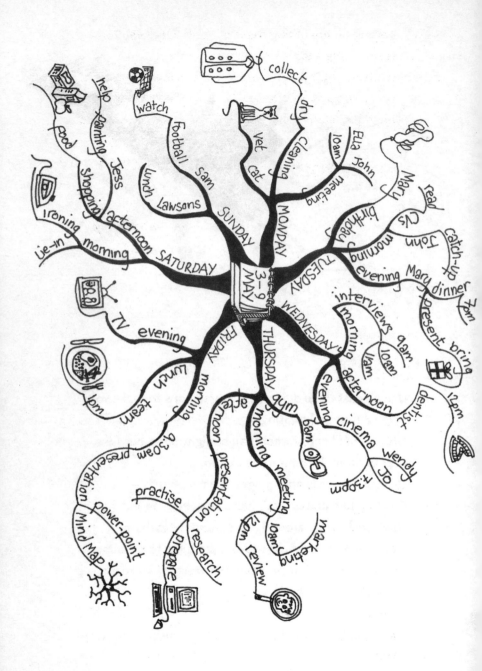

1. getting on top of that mass of notes when you're researching a topic or preparing a report
2. working out the best way to organize a complex task
3. preparing a speech or presentation
4. planning a family occasion such as a holiday or wedding

UPGRADE YOUR WORKING MEMORY

Your working memory is what you use when you want to have information to hand, ready to work with. It does not store as much data as your long-term memory, because it needs to have space available to receive the next bit of incoming information. Its capacity is still large, though – and you can upgrade it at any time with these quick-win techniques.

Memory test

To find out how good your working memory is, try this memory test. Read each series of letters, taking a second to remember each letter. Then immediately close the book and write down the letters you remember, in the correct order.

QHCY	HWTSPBC
JLQP	CBZJUWGH
KHRPS	KHRWYCV
HGRFN	WBHKPTFCS
WDMXDR	PTYRWSGCH
MWQKPD	KRTLQBXPMZ
WDPSLBM	MNBGHQWPTC

What was the longest line you remembered correctly? An average score is 5 to 7; 9 or more is in the top range. Now I don't want you to be average – I want you to be brilliant, *because you are!* Just try out the following techniques and you will find yourself improving your performance dramatically and really hitting the heights!

CHUNKING

The simplest way of boosting your memory is to 'chunk' information.

Read this imaginary mobile phone number through quickly once, taking no more than five seconds.

05964895427

Close the book immediately and try to write it down. The chances are you struggled to remember it correctly.

Now try saying the numbers to yourself in groups of three as you look at this number:

096 487 762 19

How did you do this time? The chances are you got it completely right.

This technique, called 'chunking', is very effective. The idea is to group together information you want to remember into larger, more memorable chunks. At its most basic, it is simply grouping things in small groups – groups of three are ideal.

It's not just strings of numbers you can remember like this – it's practically anything you need to hold in your working memory. Suppose you are talking to a group and you need to remember the names of all the people in it after hearing them just once:

Gemma	Hanna
Janine	Andrew
Paul	Daniel
Kylie	Ben
Rachel	Lucy
Tom	Susanna

Quite a tall order, you might think. Try repeating the names to yourself in groups of three as each person calls out his or her name and you'll find it surprisingly easy. And it works just as well with the things you have to do during the day, the names of the world's longest rivers – just about anything.

PATTERNS

You can develop the technique much more if you learn to look for patterns, especially familiar ones.

What patterns can you see in this mobile number?

01019181945

Did you see the years the two World Wars ended, 1918 and 1945? If you spotted that, you'd have no problems remembering the number. Don't worry if you didn't – the idea is to spot your own patterns. What you might see is the number of your bus to work or your best friend's birthdate.

Although patterns may not be immediately obvious, it's always worth looking for them, especially familiar patterns. Can you remember this shopping list, for instance?

bacon	tomatoes
coffee	bread
wine	cheese
cake	tea
eggs	olives
jam	

Even in chunks of three, it's not that easy. Think in terms of breakfast, tea and entertainment, and it becomes simple:

Breakfast:	**Tea:**
bacon	tea
eggs	bread
tomatoes	jam
coffee	cake

Entertainment:
olives
cheese
wine

SCHEMA

Looking for patterns works because our memories are organized in terms of what psychologists call 'schema'. A schema is a familiar pattern of relationships stored in your memory. That way they form memories so strongly linked that they are recalled more or less as a single unit.

This is so powerful that it doesn't just influence your way of remembering lists, it actually affects your entire way of thinking. In one experiment, chess grandmasters and masters were tested against ordinary chess players to see how accurately they could remember the position of 20 to 25 chess pieces placed randomly on a board after glancing at the board for 5 to 10 seconds. The masters and ordinary players were pretty similar in being able to remember the places of only 6 pieces. Yet if the pieces were arranged in the form of a game (unknown to anyone), the grandmasters and masters could suddenly remember all the positions, while the ordinary players could still manage only 6. It was clear that this was not simply a memory feat – it was due to the grandmasters' and masters' ability to see the positions as a single chunk or schema.

It is clear that the more you develop schema, or patterns, the better you'll remember things. And if you can reduce complex inputs to simple chunks, you'll find you can think about them much more clearly and effectively. As a general rule, if you ever find yourself forgetting anything, it is not because your brain is declining or your memory is receding. It's simply because you are not using the correct memory technique to help you store and retrieve the information.

NUMBER TAGS

If you have trouble remembering numbers, why not practise this technique, originally developed, like so many things, by the ancient Greeks? The idea is to link each number to a memorable image with a vaguely similar shape to the number. You can choose your own image. Here are some suggestions:

0. Doughnut
1. Paintbrush
2. Swan
3. Heart
4. Yacht
5. Hook

6. Elephant's trunk
7. Boomerang
8. Snowman
9. Flag
10. Bat and ball

To get them firmly set up in your mind, write the numbers down with your own little sketch of the images next to them.

Now if you want to remember the number 1, imagine Leonardo da Vinci holding his paintbrush up in the air. If you want to remember the number 2, you think of a swan. When you want to remember multiple numbers, combine these images into a little scenario – the more absurd and surreal, the better.

If you're always forgetting your PIN number, use this technique, and you'll remember it easily. If your PIN number is, say, 4527, think of a yacht chased by Captain Hook pursued by a swan with a boomerang in its beak. That image is so memorable you will definitely remember it! And if you know the yacht is 4, the hook is 5, the swan is 2 and the boomerang is 7, you'll be absolutely certain you have your PIN number right.

Once you've decided on the shapes to link to each number, you should stick to them all the time. If you vary them, you may find yourself becoming confused.

To help you to remember your number tags:

- **Draw a Mind Map for the numbers with each of the images on its own branch.**
- **Practise throughout the day with any numbers you see — prices in shops or today's date, for example.**

RHYME TAGS

You can also choose your image using rhymes, for instance:

0.	Hero	6. Sticks
1.	Bun	7. Heaven
2.	Shoe	8. Skate
3.	Tree	9. Vine
4.	Door	10. Hen
5.	Hive	

USING YOUR TAGS

Once you've got your number images firmly in your head, you can use them to help you remember all kinds of things. You'll be amazed by how effective it is.

Try this memory test first to see how you get on without these tags. Spend one minute going through this shopping list trying to remember each item:

1. Buns	6. Mayonnaise
2. Soap	7. Garlic
3. Salt	8. Apples
4. Oats	9. Vinegar
5. Mustard	10. Eggs

Forget about it for 15 minutes. Then try to write the list down with the items in the right order and check how well you did. Most people manage 7 right at most – often with a mistake or two in the order.

Now try the same with another list. This time, spend the minute making vivid connections between the object and your number image:

1. Bread	6. Potatoes
2. Bleach	7. Eggs
3. Tea	8. Soap
4. Salt	9. Binbags
5. Milk	10. Detergent

Make the connections as lively and weird as possible. With bread, you might think of Leonardo da Vinci slicing a loaf with a paintbrush. Absurd as it is, you won't forget it! With the bleach, you might think of trying to bleach a paint-stained swan to get its feathers white again. With the tea, you might think of teacups balancing on a heart!

Again, forget about it for 15 minutes. Then try writing down the list again. This time you are, amazingly, likely to get it 100 per cent right all the items in the right order. What's more, you'll find you still get it right if you test yourself the next day, or even a month afterwards.

ALPHABET TAGS

Numbers are not the only things you can use to make tags. Any familiar sequence will work in the same way, such as the alphabet. There is an example of alphabet tags below. These tags sound like the letter they are attached to, as it makes it easier to remember them, hence 'Ace' for 'A'. The tag 'Art', for example, would not work as you don't hear the letter 'A' when you say it.

A. Ace	N. Entrance
B. Bee	O. Ocean
C. Sea	P. Pea
D. Delilah	Q. Queue
E. Easel	R. Artist
F. Effigy	S. Espresso
G. Genes	T. Tepee
H. H-beam	U. Youth
I. Eye	V. Venus
J. Jade	W. WC
K. Cake	X. X-ray
L. Elk	Y. Wipe
M. Embrace	Z. Zebra

To help you to remember your alphabet tags:

- **Try learning the letters in groups of four (a kind of chunking).**
- **Make up a little tune for them, similar to the way you learned your ABC, only use the words for the letters for the song and not the letters themselves, for example 'Ace, Bee, Sea ...'**

Once you have memorized the tags you can put the system into practice.

Imagine that you want to memorize the following list of words:

A. Kite	N. Tomato
B. Hilarious	O. Calculator
C. Book	P. Glass
D. Fairy	Q. Mobile phone
E. Stiletto	R. Umbrella
F. Glove	S. Spaghetti
G. Plant	T. Pencil
H. Radiator	U. Grapes
I. Coat hook	V. Chef
J. Vase	W. Rose
K. Office	X. Window
L. Chocolate	Y. Stone
M. Desk	Z. Fan

You will remember them easily if you link each of the images in turn to your alphabet tag. The first on the list is 'Kite' and the first letter of the alphabet is 'A'. Your tag for this is 'Ace', so imagine flying a huge brightly coloured ace-shaped kite in the air. The more imaginative and exaggerated the image you conjure up in your mind, the easier it will be to remember it. Try to get as many of your senses involved as possible – can you imagine the sound of the ace-shaped kite flapping in the wind?

The second word on the list is 'Hilarious'. Your alphabet tag for the letter 'B' is a bee, so this time you could imagine a bee flying around crazily buzzing with laughter.

Go through the remaining words in the list and see how you would tag them to your alphabet tags.

REMEMBERING NAMES AND FACES

Has this kind of thing ever happened to you? You run into someone you met only yesterday, and with whom you had a great conversation. You turn to introduce this person to your friend and realize with embarrassment that you've forgotten his or her name. If so, you're not alone. However, there are a number of ways you can dramatically improve your ability to put a name to a face.

First of all, you can make the task easier by making sure you get the name of the person you're being introduced to properly in the first place. If you don't hear a name clearly, ask for it to be repeated. Then say it back to the person to help it stick in your mind and then use it in conversation as often as you feel comfortable.

Secondly, you can create vivid mental images. Usually, if you can't remember someone's name it is because you are not using your imagination to help you, or are not making a strong enough association. As you listen to the name, try to find a visual link between the person's face and his or her name. If a man's name is Brown and he has brown hair, the link is obvious. If there is not an obvious link, you need to make one. It doesn't have to be right or logical or even flattering. The more absurd, and therefore memorable, the better. Create a quick cartoon image of the person's face, exaggerating distinctive features. He or she might have a big nose, for instance, or dark eyebrows. Then try to find a link between the feature and name. If you meet someone with a big nose whose name is Mark

Bentley, visualize the magnificent nose of a pink Bentley. It doesn't matter that the person's nose isn't really like that. It simply combines the face and name into a memorable image.

With practice this becomes second nature and you can do it in a split-second.

BEAT ABSENT-MINDEDNESS BY BEING PRESENT MINDED

How many times have you spent ages hunting for something you had in your hand just moments ago, or wandered into another room without quite knowing why you're there? We tend to call all this 'absent-mindedness' and assume it is a memory problem. In fact, such lapses are often nothing to do with memory; they are usually failures of *attention*.

The solution is to pay more attention and be 'present-minded'. It requires a little more effort at first – you really do need to concentrate and plan to remember. You'll soon find it pays off and becomes second nature.

First, get into the habit of momentarily pausing for thought. When you hear the phone ring, don't just drop your pen and run to answer it. Take a split second to make a mental image of where you put the pen down. When you come in and put your keys down, again take a split second to form a mental image, noting where you put them down. In the same way, when you leave somewhere, take just a moment to scan around to make sure you have remembered everything.

The second key strategy is planning. Quite often you forget things simply because you haven't planned. As you try to work out all you're supposed to do and remember amidst the chaos, your working memory is trying to hold on to so many things that it overloads – and then, of course, you forget things. Indeed, it becomes a vicious circle, as the fear of forgetting makes you panicky, reducing the efficiency of your working memory! What proper planning does is mimimize the number of things you need to hold in your working memory and so free your mind to calmly cope with the present.

Some planning tips:

1. Try to think ahead. Set things out for the next morning before you go to bed.
2. Set aside time for planning. Get up 15 minutes earlier, for instance, to set out your tasks for the day clearly or talk them through with your partner.
3. Think a task through clearly before you embark on it.
4. Take time to write things in a Mind Map diary.
5. Write yourself reminder notes in prominent places.

MNEMONICS

Over the centuries people have devised all kinds of techniques to help them remember things. One of the most effective of these mnemonics is to turn the thing into a story or a sentence.

Acronyms

Acronyms use the initial letter of each item to be remembered to create a sentence. Once, at school, children were told how to remember the order of the seven major colours in the rainbow – red, orange, yellow, green, blue, indigo, violet – with the acronymn 'Richard of York Gave Battle in Vain'. You can make up your own acronym for anything you want to remember. Maybe you can't remember all the names of your nephews and nieces, or your grandchildren. If one of the families you want to remember is Sandy and Peter and their children Andrew, Daniel and Elizabeth, why not call them the SPADEs? If the children are in age order, so much the better – otherwise, make an anagram of the initial letters. If all the names begin with consonants, imagine vowels to make your word.

Rhymes

Rhymes are another useful mnemonic. In the days when stories were passed down orally, people used rhymes to help them remember, because like sounds are stored together in your brain and reinforce each other. Simple rhymes were used, like this famous one to remember the number of days in the months:

Thirty days have September,
April, June and November.
All the rest have thirty-one
Excepting February alone,
Which has twenty-eight days clear
Or twenty-nine days in a leap year.

And if you want to remember all the kings and queens of England in order, there's a variety of rhymes like this:

Willie, Willie, Harry One
Steve and Harry, Dick and John
Harry, Edwards One, Two, Three
Richard Two, then Harrys three
Edwards Four, Five, Dick (the bad)
Harrys (twain), Ned Six (the lad),
Mary, Bessie, James you ken
Then Charlie, Charlie, James again ...
Will and Mary, Anna Gloria,
Georges four, Will Four, Victoria;
Edward Seven next and then
Comes George the Fifth in 1910;
Ned the Eight soon abdicated
Then Georgie Six was coronated
After which, Elizabeth
And that's all, folks – until her death ...

These rhymes are well known. If you like, though, you can make up your own for any list or collection of things you want to remember.

USING FIRST AND LAST

We tend to remember the things we heard or saw first better than anything else in an event. If there is any moment you recall vividly from a piece of music, it is the opening. And how many people remember the first line of a novel and none other? We also tend to remember recent events better than those which are longer ago. We remember yesterday better than the day before, last week better than a fortnight ago, and so on. And we remember the last things on a list better than those that came before.

So we remember the first and last better than the things that come in between. This is well worth remembering when you're trying to learn something.

ARISTOTLE'S LAWS

The brilliant Greek philosopher Aristotle realized the power of association in learning 2,500 years ago. Aristotle realized that we learn things and build up complex ideas simply by linking two or more simple observations together. He identified three laws of association:

1. Contiguity   3. Contrast
2. Similarity

By contiguity, Aristotle meant things occurring near each other. If Sarah always arrives at work just after Paul, for instance, the two become associated in your mind.

With similarity, he was talking about how we associate things that look or sound alike. If two people walk into the office with similar haircuts, you will make the link.

With contrast, Aristotle was talking about how opposites are linked, like day and night, black and white, men and women, up and down.

METHOD OF LOCI

By far the most powerful and adaptable way of developing your memory through using association is the method of loci. This makes powerful links between and organizes each of the items to be remembered, so that the order is remembered too.

The method of loci was first described by the Ancient Greek poet Simonides, who needed powerful memory techniques to enable him to remember huge chunks of epic poetry for recital. The story goes that he got the idea for it when he was invited to a banquet at the house of the nobleman Scopias to recite a poem in the host's honour. Moments after he had finished the poem and left the room, the roof of the hall collapsed, killing all inside. The bodies were so badly mangled that they were hard to recognize. Simonides had a clear memory of who had been sitting where, and was able to identify the bodies for the distraught relatives.

The method of loci makes the most of the fact that our spatial memory – our memory for where things are – is usually much better than any other, perhaps because our memories evolved in the first place to help us find our way through the wild and to locate food stores.

To see how true this is, try answering these questions:

- **How many chairs do you have at home?**
- **How many times have you seen your best friend in the last month?**
- **Which is furthest from London – Rome or Warsaw?**

The chances are that in order to answer these questions, you tried to scan through your own visual route through the events. The method of loci takes advantage of this natural tendency. This is the technique used by most memory champions to achieve seemingly miraculous feats of memory.

The idea is to take a route you know really well, then in your imagination link the objects you want to remember to places along the route. Simonides advised against using places that were too dark or too bright, because this might obscure the object you want to remember.

The places you could select might be on your route to work, for instance:

1. Your hallway
2. Your front door
3. The pavement outside
4. The street corner
5. The grocer's shop
6. The newspaper stall
7. The bus stop
8. The bus
9. The stop where you get off
10. The tower block

The advantage of using a route like this is that you can select as many points along it as things you want to remember.

Now you link the things to remember to the places on your route with as clear an image as you can muster.

Say you needed to remember things to do for your best friend's wedding – write a speech, hire top hat and tailcoat, buy flowers, cancel the papers, borrow a car and get the ring from the groom. For writing a speech, you could imagine yourself sitting on the floor in the middle of your hall with a big piece of paper in your hand, ready to draw a Mind Map. For hiring a top hat, you could imagine yourself doffing an enormous top hat to a beautiful lady. For the flowers, you could imagine the pavement outside your door strewn with thousands of flowers.

Once you have these images, make sure they are firmly fixed in your head by going through your journey to work in your head, checking the items in their places on the way.

And what about that speech you have to make at the wedding? How effective it will be if you can do it apparently off-the-cuff, using the method of loci and imagination to remember all the main points? (Another way would be to use a Mind Map; see page 56. A Mind Map is simply a network of locations, associations and key images.)

A MEMORY MIND MAP

Now you've learned several different quick-win techniques for boosting your memory, why not bring them all together in a Mind Map? This will help you to remember them all and give you a quick visual reference you can use in an instant whenever you need it – it will also help you hone your Mind Mapping skills.

1. Gather all the materials you need – an array of coloured pens and a large blank sheet of paper.
2. Turn your paper sideways and let your ideas expand in all directions.
3. Draw a simple image or symbol to represent your central idea – in this case you could draw a brain to symbolize your memory.
4. Then think of the various memory techniques you've just learned.
5. As you think about each one, write a key word or draw a simple image to illustrate it – numbers for number tags perhaps, or a front door for your method of loci – and link it to your central idea with a line.

You can use this Mind Map to help you select memory techniques as you work through The 7-Day Get Sharp Plan. This is coming up next and it will really improve your brain fitness! Are you ready for it? To prepare yourself, look back over these quick-win techniques once more and briefly run through each one again. One great advantage of all these methods is that the more you use them, the more reliable your memory becomes, thus improving your mental powers as you progress through life.

Now for The 7-Day Get Sharp Plan – get ready to get your brain juices flowing!

Chapter 4

The 7-Day Get Sharp Plan

As soon as you start using the key memory techniques in Chapter 3 you will notice that it is easier to remember everything. This is because the techniques work *with* your brain and how it likes to work, not against it. For the next 7 days you need to practise using these techniques until they become second nature. The techniques alone will improve your ability to remember things, and they will also work their magic in others ways: they will flex your brain power and automatically move your brain fitness to a new level. Your brain benefits just as much as your body from a good workout. The more you challenge your brain, the more you encourage it to build new connections and stimulate the flow of blood to it.

The 7-Day Get Sharp Plan is designed to fit comfortably into your everyday life. The sessions only last for an hour each and to get the most benefit out of them you should set aside a solid hour. If you really are too busy to do this, you can also break up each session into two half-hour or four 15-minute sessions (each session is conveniently divided into four 15-minute sections).

As you work through each session, resist the temptation to cheat. By that I mean allowing yourself a little longer over the exercise, peaking at the answers before you should or bending the rules – yes, even a little! They are only short exercises and being disciplined with yourself really pays off. There are tips in each section to help you select the memory techniques you might find most useful to assist you. However, do feel free to choose any of the quick-win techniques from Chapter 3 as there is really no right or wrong way of doing the sessions – it's about what works for you.

What you need

All you need for each of the daily sessions is:

1. An ordinary pencil or pen
2. Four or five coloured pens (for Mind Maps)
3. Paper
4. A watch or stopwatch to time yourself to the second (most mobile phones have a stopwatch)
5. Your full attention!

Sharpen up – DAY 1

Total time: 60 minutes

PART 1

BRAIN PRIMER
Time: 15 minutes (including time for checking answers)

MEMORY TONER

Time: 60 seconds
Focus: Short-term memory

What's the word?
Study this list of words for 60 seconds. Cover the book and see how many you can remember:

1. Harvest
2. Rafter
3. Chicken
4. Absolution
5. Present
6. Generous
7. Apricot
8. Nebulous
9. Impressive
10. Jasper

TIP: Try using number rhyme or number shapes (see page 66) to remember the list of words. For example, with number rhyme, the number one is linked with the rhyming word 'bun'. In this instance you could link 'bun' with 'harvest' by imagining a vast field of golden wheat being harvested and made into a piping hot bun. Hear the rustle of the wheat, smell the freshly baked bread, taste the soft juicy bread! Really get all your senses on board to fix it in your memory.

MEMORY BUILDING

Time: 120 seconds
Focus: Long-term memory

Daughters of memory

The nine muses were the goddesses of Ancient Greek myth who ruled over the arts and sciences and gave artists inspiration. They were the daughters of Zeus and Mnemosyne, the goddess of memory who gave us the word mnemonics. Memory was crucial because in the times before books, poets carried their works and learning in their heads.

Take 60 seconds to learn them. Cover up the book. Write down the names of all the muses.

Calliope: the muse of epic poetry
Clio: the muse of history
Erato: the muse of love poetry
Euterpe: the muse of music
Melpomene: the muse of tragedy
Polyhymnia: the muse of sacred poetry
Terpsichore: the muse of dance
Thalia: the muse of comedy
Urania: the muse of astronomy

Check your answers. Now give yourself 60 seconds to remember the skill of each muse. Cover up the book and write down the muses with their field of inspiration.

WORD POWER

Time: 60 seconds
Focus: Language

Phrase round the edge
Think radiantly to work out what these odd ways of displaying common phrases mean. The first is worked out for you.

    i i
    bag bag

This stands for bags under your eyes. Now try these:

1. ecar
2. £££
   delivery
3. 7.15 just a.m.

4. taking meas
5. ga me
6. i'm
   moon

LOGIC BOOSTER

Time: 30 seconds
Focus: Logic skills

Age-old logic

15 years ago, I was a third of my mother's age, now I'm half. How old am I?

TIP: Try using algebra: let my age be x and my mother's age be y.

ANALYTIC POWER

Time: 30 seconds
Focus: Logic skills

Odd one out

Which of these is the odd one out?

Willow	Minimum
Noon	Turbot
Beelzebub	Comic
Eglantine	Destined
Stars	Loyal
Mummy	

TIP: Look for patterns.

CREATIVE THINKING

Time: 180 seconds
Focus: Logic skills

Global warming
Most scientists are now agreed that atmospheric pollution is making the world's climate warmer. Think of as many different strategies as you can to avert the crisis.

TIP: Draw a quick sketch of a Mind Map. Start with an image in the centre of the page, for example a big thermometer stuck in planet earth, and add to it four or five main branches with key ideas, such as 'causes', 'effects' and 'solutions', and explore each of these with sub-branches. Remember to use your coloured pens as colour helps set your imagination on fire. (See page 57 for more help drawing a Mind Map.)

PART 2

SKILL DEVELOPING

Time: 15 minutes
There is no better way of establishing new connections throughout your brain than learning a new skill, especially a musical skill (see the Mozart effect, page 33). This improves your ability to think and reason in space and time. What's more, it helps make thinking pleasurable, which in turn rewards your brain with dopamine, itself a crucial ingredient for age-proofing your brain.

You've probably noticed that when you first start learning a new skill, such as riding a bike, playing snooker, driving a car or playing the guitar, it usually requires a good deal of mental effort. This is because your brain needs to form new and different synapses and neural assemblies to do it. However, once you master the routine, the mental effort you need to put in diminishes. The more you practise your new higher skill, the more automatic it becomes until the new neuron networks you have built up to learn it are freed up for other tasks. This is why learning to master a new skill gives your brain such a boost.

Your next task is to practise intensively a skill for 15 minutes, ideally something musical. The exercise below is a music-based brain booster. Feel free to choose your own skill if you prefer.

Music test

Try and work out what these famous tunes are from the sequence of notes alone. If you have access to a musical instrument, play the first two notes only. Work the remaining notes out by humming them to yourself:

1. C E G G– G G E E
2. G F F–A B Csharp D E F E D D–
3. D D A A A E F E D
4. E F G A G A D C A G F D

TIP: If you aren't a musical person and can't imagine what the notes would sound like, look up the answers on page 332. Return to the list of notes and go through them one by one, humming the tune to yourself. Instead of singing the words, sing the note given, trying to hear its pitch. Practise this again and again for 15 minutes until you can.

PART 3
BRAIN STRETCHER QUIZ

Time: 15 minutes

Quizzes are tests of your semantic memory. They are immensely popular and fun and also a great way to exercise your brain, especially if you do them against the clock. This is because they push you to search your memory banks and improve your ability to recall information. There are few better ways to keep your brain in trim than joining a local quiz team. There are of course countless quiz books available and many good quiz programmes on TV. In the meanwhile, here is one to get you going. Give yourself no more than 10 minutes to answer all the questions. Tick the right answer.

TIP: If you can't answer one of the questions, don't dwell on it. Move on to the next one and come back to it at the end of the quiz. Your brain will subconsciously work on the question whilst you turn your attention to the others and you may well find that you have the right answer by the time you come back to it.

1. Which famous band were originally known as the Quarrymen?

- [ ] The Rolling Stones
- [ ] The Beatles
- [ ] The Animals
- [ ] The Stone Roses

2. What is the longest river in the Americas?

- [ ] Mississippi
- [ ] Orinoco
- [ ] Colorado
- [ ] Amazon

3. Who painted the ceiling of the Sistine Chapel?

- [ ] Leonardo
- [ ] Michelangelo
- [ ] Raphael
- [ ] Titian

4. Who plays the part of Harry Potter in the films?

- [ ] Leonardo di Caprio
- [ ] Orlando Bloom
- [ ] Rupert Grint
- [ ] Daniel Radcliffe

5. What is the capital of Romania?

- [ ] Belgrade
- [ ] Budapest
- [ ] Bucharest
- [ ] Sofia

6. In which country is the temple of Angkor Wat?

- [ ] Laos
- [ ] Vietnam
- [ ] Cambodia
- [ ] Thailand

7. Which of these parts of the body has not been transplanted?

- [ ] Liver
- [ ] Hand
- [ ] Face
- [ ] Chest

8. What city was once known as Byzantium?

- [ ] Beirut
- [ ] Rome
- [ ] Alexandria
- [ ] Istanbul

9. Where would you find the Traitors' Gate?

- [ ] Hermitage, St Petersburg
- [ ] Bastille, Paris
- [ ] The Tower of London
- [ ] Berlin

10. Which suffragette threw herself under the King's horse in 1913?

- [ ] Emily Mortimer
- [ ] Emily Pankhurst
- [ ] Emily Davison
- [ ] Emily Robinson

11. In which Charles Dickens novel does Miss Havisham appear?

- [ ] *Bleak House*
- [ ] *Hard Times*
- [ ] *Great Expectations*
- [ ] *David Copperfield*

12. What is the particle of electromagnetic radiation?

- [ ] Proton
- [ ] Photon
- [ ] Electron
- [ ] Neutron

13. Who wrote *Agnes Grey*?

- [ ] Charlotte Brontë
- [ ] Anne Brontë
- [ ] Emily Brontë
- [ ] Branwell Brontë

14. Which of these presidents was not assassinated?

- [ ] Jackson
- [ ] Lincoln
- [ ] Garfield
- [ ] Kennedy

15. What does PDA stand for?

- [ ] Police Database Access
- [ ] Personal Digital Assistant
- [ ] Private Detective Agency
- [ ] Personal Development Aid

16. What is the scientific name for the group of animals that includes garden snails?

- [ ] Arthropod
- [ ] Gastropod
- [ ] Amphibia
- [ ] Mollusca

17. In which city would you find the Bronze Horseman?

- [ ] St Petersburg
- [ ] Paris
- [ ] Vienna
- [ ] Madrid

18. Who wrote a diary about her experiences under the Nazis in Amsterdam?

- [ ] Lillian Hellman
- [ ] Anna Gardner
- [ ] Ingrid Bergman
- [ ] Anne Frank

19. What is the highest waterfall in the world?

- [ ] Victoria Falls
- [ ] Niagara Falls
- [ ] Iguacu Falls
- [ ] Angel Falls

20. What does MRI stand for?

- [ ] Magnetic Resonance Imaging
- [ ] Manchester Royal Infirmary
- [ ] Meat Recovery Initiative
- [ ] Multiple Respiratory Infection

21. Which one of these is a major ore for iron?

- [ ] Hematite
- [ ] Bauxite
- [ ] Carbonite
- [ ] Limonite

22. What do isobars show?

- [ ] Lines of equal pressure
- [ ] Lines of equal temperature
- [ ] Areas of equal magnetic intensity
- [ ] Areas of equal gravitational force

23. Which of these is not a moon of Jupiter?

- [ ] Europa
- [ ] Io
- [ ] Titan
- [ ] Callisto

24. Which city was destroyed by a volcano in AD 79?

- [ ] Sidon
- [ ] Carthage
- [ ] Rome
- [ ] Pompeii

25. Which famous writer was married to Marilyn Monroe?

- [ ] Arthur Miller
- [ ] Arthur Haley
- [ ] Scott Fitzgerald
- [ ] Tennessee Williams

26. Who are the world's most profitable food sellers?

- [ ] Carrefours
- [ ] Nestlé
- [ ] Wal-Mart
- [ ] Kraft

27. What was the name of the aircraft that dropped the atomic bomb on Hiroshima?

- [ ] Fat Boy
- [ ] Fat Man
- [ ] Enola Gay
- [ ] Charlie Parker

28. What is the highest mountain in Africa?

- [ ] Cotopaxi
- [ ] Mount Kenya
- [ ] Ruwenzori
- [ ] Kilimanjaro

29. Who did Zinedine Zidane headbutt in the 2006 World Cup Final?

- [ ] Materazzi
- [ ] Maserati
- [ ] Del Piero
- [ ] Cannavaro

30. Which famous novelist was played by Nicole Kidman in the film *The Hours*?

- [ ] Katherine Mansfield
- [ ] Jane Austen
- [ ] Virginia Woolf
- [ ] Iris Murdoch

31. Who was the first king of Persia?

- [ ] Alexander the Great
- [ ] Cyrus the Great
- [ ] Darius the Great
- [ ] Xerxes

32. What part of the brain is named after a seahorse?

- [ ] Cortex
- [ ] Cerebellum
- [ ] Corpus callosum
- [ ] Hippocampus

33. Which geological era saw the dinosaurs at their height?

- [ ] Carboniferous
- [ ] Triassic
- [ ] Permian
- [ ] Jurassic

34. Which of these rivers is not in Russia?

- [ ] Ob
- [ ] Weser
- [ ] Lena
- [ ] Yenesei

35. Which substance was used for the first operation under general anaesthetic?

- [ ] Chloroform
- [ ] Nitrous Oxide
- [ ] Ether
- [ ] Alcohol

36. What is the capital of Tajikistan?

- [ ] Bishkek
- [ ] Ashgabat
- [ ] Dushanbe
- [ ] Akmola

37. Which of these organizations deals with world science?

- [ ] UNICEF
- [ ] UNESCO
- [ ] UCLA
- [ ] UAEA

38. Who had a hit with 'Where is the Love?'

- [ ] R. Kelly
- [ ] Usher
- [ ] Big Brovaz
- [ ] Black Eyed Peas

39. Which is thought to be Shakespeare's last play?

- [ ] *The Winter's Tale*
- [ ] *King Lear*
- [ ] *The Tempest*
- [ ] *Richard III*

40. Where was the assassination that triggered World War I?

- [ ] Sarajevo
- [ ] Budapest
- [ ] Sofia
- [ ] Moscow

41. What is measured with red shift?

- [ ] The rotation speed of an atom
- [ ] Heat radiation
- [ ] A star's luminosity
- [ ] The movement of a galaxy

42. Which famous French scientist was guillotined?

- [ ] Pasteur
- [ ] Ampère
- [ ] Lavoisier
- [ ] Fresnel

43. What is the colour of visible light with the shortest wavelength?

- [ ] Red
- [ ] Indigo
- [ ] Violet
- [ ] Blue

44. What is the largest thing that ever lived?

- [ ] Balaenoptera musculus
- [ ] Sequoiadendron giganteum
- [ ] Argentinosaurus huinculensis
- [ ] Tyrannosaurus rex

45. Where would you find the Mare Fecunditatis?

- [ ] In a woman's reproductive system
- [ ] In a Roman bath-house
- [ ] In Australia
- [ ] On the Moon

PART 4

MENTAL CUSHION: RELAXATION

Time: 15 minutes

Chapter 7 looks in detail at the benefits of relaxing and creating regular mental space in your day. I cannot overemphasize the importance of building in time to rest and relax EVERY DAY – even if it is only for a few minutes of deep breathing. This is because resting your brain is just as important as giving it a good workout. When you relax, your brain files away information it has received so it can easily access it again. It's a bit like cataloguing books in an enormous library – if you simply leave the books in a big messy heap you'll find it extremely hard to find a particular volume when you need it. Give your brain the chance to rest and you will empower it to concentrate and perform to perfection.

Part of your daily mental makeover is relaxing for 15 minutes at the end of every session. Make sure you set aside this time, even if you have to wait until later in the day, as it's actually a key part of keeping your mind in tip-top condition.

1. Find a quiet, comfortable space where you won't be disturbed. Lie on your back with your arms by your sides or sit down with your arms and legs unfolded.
2. Concentrate on breathing slowly and deeply, in through your nose and out through your mouth.
3. Focus on a spot on the ceiling or wall opposite.
4. Begin to count backwards from 10 to 1 very slowly.
5. Close your eyes and move down through your body mentally from head to toe, silently telling each part to relax completely as you do.
6. Now imagine a special calm, comfortable place, such as a beautiful sunken garden, or a heated pool in a tropical paradise at sunset.
7. Imagine walking down ten steps into the garden or pool, counting each step carefully as you go.
8. When you've reached the bottom, look around you and try to imagine the beautiful, relaxing sensations you feel as you do.

9. Now picture yourself dealing with everything you do in a calm, confident, relaxed fashion. Imagine it in as much detail as you possibly can.

10. Repeat the previous step several times, each time finishing by saying to yourself, 'I am always calm and confident.'

11. Finally, when you are finished, count slowly down from 10 to 1, telling yourself it's time to re-enter your day.

12. Continue to lie or sit where you are for a few more minutes breathing slowly and deeply. Open your eyes feeling calm and confident.

Sharpen up – DAY 2

Total time: 60 minutes

PART 1

BRAIN PRIMER

Time: 15 minutes (including time for checking answers)

MEMORY TONER

Time: 60 seconds
Focus: Short-term memory

What's the word?
Study this list of words. Cover the book and see how many you can remember:

Appetite	Modem
Betrothal	Omnipotent
Buttress	Perspiration
Cherry	Pipeline
Cottage	Riff
Fibre optic	Slender
Interval	Succulent
Invasion	Sweetness
Marquee	Waterfall

TIP: Try Linking to alphabet tags (see page 69). For example, the tag for 'W' is WC. To link 'W' to 'Waterfall' you could imagine a great white, foaming waterfall pouring into a toilet from a great height. Hear the thundering sound of the water as it tumbles down, feel the mist of the water on your face as you stand beside it! Again, really let your imagination run wild – the more playful you are with the images the easier it will be to remember them.

MEMORY BUILDING

Time: 120 seconds
Focus: Long-term memory

Fact bank

To avoid confusion, many scientists and engineers around the world use a universal system of measurements called the SI (Système International d'Unitiés). There are seven basic units from which all others derive.

Take 60 seconds to learn them. Cover up the book. Write down the names of all the units.

metre: unit of length	kelvin: unit of temperature
kilogram: unit of mass	candela: unit of brightness
second: unit of time	mole: unit of substance
ampere: unit of electric current	

TIP: Try an acronym (see page 75).

Check your answers. Take 60 seconds to learn what the seven units measure. Cover up the book and write them down.

TIP: Try a vivid visual link (see page 72).

WORD POWER

Time: 60 seconds
Focus: Language

Word ladders

Lewis Carroll, the creator of *Alice in Wonderland,* created this puzzle in 1878. The idea is to change the word at the top to the word at the bottom, changing one letter at a time to create a new word on each rung.

CAT   COG
COT   DOG

Now fill in the blanks with these:

WARM   ——
——   COLD
——

GIVE   ——
——   TAKE
——

GRASS   ——

         ——   TREES

         ——

TIP: You may have to use new letters that are not in the final word.

LOGIC BOOSTER

Time: 60 seconds
Focus: Logic skills

Seating arrangements
Six friends, Julia, Susan, Robin, Paul, George and David, go to the theatre. Unfortunately, they cannot all sit in the same row. Instead, they are spread over four rows:

> Julia's partner is sitting on her left
> Paul's view is blocked by Robin
> Robin's sister is sitting with David in the same seat number
>   as Julia
> George is alone in the third row
>
> Where is everybody sitting?

TIP: Number the four rows and start by entering the person whose position is clearly stated.

ANALYTIC POWER

Time: 4 minutes
Focus: Logic skills

Three houses, three needs

There are three houses that need to be supplied with three utility services, namely water, gas and electricity. Each house needs to be connected to all three utilities, which means that each house will have three lines and that each utility will have three lines. The challenge is to connect them without crossing lines through houses or utilities. The houses cannot share lines either. Draw the nine lines connecting the three houses and three utilities.

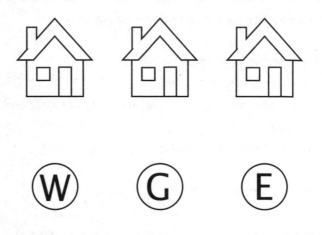

TIP: Try solving it in 3D rather than 2D.

CREATIVE THINKING

Time: 180 seconds
Focus: Logic skills

Multiple uses

At the beginning of the book in the 7-Minute Mind Makeover you had to find as many uses as possible for a penknife. This time try and think of as many uses as possible for a chocolate button. Again, be as crazy with your ideas as you like – chocolate buttons are not just for eating! For example, you could thread hundreds of them on to very long pieces of string and use them to cordon off lanes in a chocolate swimming pool.

TIP: Draw a quick Mind Map to brainstorm your ideas, starting with an image of a chocolate button at the centre.

PART 2

SKILL DEVELOPING

Time: 15 minutes

As in the first session, your next task is to practise your chosen skill for 15 minutes.

Music test

Try and work out what these famous tunes are from the sequence of notes alone. If you have access to a musical instrument, play the first two notes only. Work the remaining notes out by humming them to yourself:

1. G–DC–BAGFG–C–BAGFG
2. ECE–DCDECAE
3. EEEEFGAG– EFGAA–GCGFE

TIP: As before, if you don't guess the tune quickly, look up the answer on page 333. Now try working through the list of notes given one by one, humming the tune to yourself. Don't sing the words, sing the note given, trying to hear its pitch. Practise this again and again for 15 minutes until you get the notes perfectly in your head.

PART 3

DAYDREAMING

Time: 15 minutes

Daydreaming is a crucial part of toning your brain since it allows your imagination to take over and flex its creative muscles. Your imagination plays a key part in helping you to remember whatever you choose.

Spend the next 15 minutes daydreaming about what you would like to be experiencing in 10 years' time. Think about all aspects of what you would like to be experiencing, the people you would like to be with, the places you would like to see, the new skills you would like to be practising, the foods you would like to be eating. Get all of your senses on board – feel the sun on your face if you'd like to be in a warm, sunny climate – and let your brain take you on a vivid imaginary adventure.

PART 4

MENTAL CUSHION: RELAXATION

Time: 15 minutes

Find a comfortable space where you won't be disturbed and spend 15 minutes practising the relaxation technique from yesterday on page 102.

Sharpen up – DAY 3

Total time: 60 minutes

PART 1

BRAIN PRIMER

Time: 15 minutes (including time for checking answers)

MEMORY TONER

Time: 120 seconds
Focus: Short-term memory

Number punching
Give yourself 60 seconds to remember as many numbers as possible from the list below. Cover up the book and write down your answers.

4567	36378492
3756	373839309
23564	767483827
58347	3756392011
365764	1293980930
253498	45363448411
3782745	28394836329
4625928	027236817281
29478456	126351546298

TIP: Try Chunking (page 62).

MEMORY BUILDING

Time: 120 seconds
Focus: Long-term memory

Fact bank

Take 60 seconds to learn all the presidents of the USA since World War II, in order. Cover up the book. Write down the names.

1945–1953	Harry S Truman
1953–1961	Dwight D Eisenhower
1961–1963	John F Kennedy
1963–1969	Lyndon B Johnson
1969–1974	Richard Nixon
1974–1977	Gerald Ford
1977–1981	Jimmy Carter
1981–1989	Ronald Reagan
1989–1993	George Bush senior
1993–2001	Bill Clinton
2001–	George Bush junior

Check your answers. Take 60 seconds to learn the dates for each. Cover the book up. Write down the full list of presidents with dates. Check your answers.

TIP: With complex memory tasks like this, it is worth looking for patterns or 'landmarks' to act as a framework for memories and to add meaning. Presidents usually serve four or eight years. Learn just the start dates for those presidents who served eight years first (Truman 45, Eisenhower 53, Reagan 81, Clinton 93), then those that served four years (Carter 77, George Bush senior 89). In between Eisenhower and Carter came four presidents who did not serve full terms. Kennedy became president in 1961 and was assassinated after just 2 years in office, to be replaced by Johnson for the remainder of this eight-year block, while Nixon (president from 1969) served 5 years before he was impeached to let Ford take over for the remaining 3 years of this eight-year block.

WORD POWER

Time: 120 seconds
Focus: Language

Crossed love

Here are some mixed up 2-line quotations from famous love poems. Your task is to sort them out and put them into the correct order.

Love is not love
That's newly sprung in June.
How do I love thee? Let me count the ways.
O, my luve is like a red, red rose,
That alters when it alteration finds
Than to have never loved at all.

Thou art more lovely and more temperate:
Shall I compare thee to a summer's day?
Like the night of cloudless climes and starry skies;
I have spread my dreams under your feet;
She walks in beauty,
It's better to have loved and lost
Tread softly because you tread on my dreams.

LOGIC BOOSTER

Time: 120 seconds
Focus: Logic skills

Food for thought
Solve these logic problems:

When starting her diet, Louise weighs 75 kg. She aims to lose 16 per cent of her weight. What does she want to weigh?

It costs a farmer £45 to feed 100 chickens for 9 days. How much will it cost him to feed 150 chickens for a week?

Working at the dogs' home, you've been given a big box of dog food weighing 12 kg. You must feed one portion every day to each of six dogs for the next ten days. How big must each portion be?

TIP: With the second two questions, simplify the problem by working out the daily consumption.

ANALYTIC POWER

Time: 120 seconds
Focus: Logic skills

Morse code

Morse code was developed by American Samuel Morse in the 1840s to send messages over the electric telegraph he invented in 1836. The idea was that the electrical signals would punch marks on paper tapes in either dots or dashes. Today, because of the huge advances in communications technology, Morse code is only used for a handful of emergency and specialized uses, such as for navigational radio beacons, amateur radio operators and land mobile transmitter identification.

The code below is the first message ever sent. Use the key below to work out what was said:

.- - .... .- -/- -. - - - -../.... .- – ..../.- - -. .- - - ..- - -. .... -/

Here are the letters for Morse code

A .-	I ..	Q - -.-	Y -.- -
B -...	J .- - -	R .-.	Z - -..
C -.-.	K -.-	S ...	Full stop .-.-.-
D -..	L .-..	T -	Comma - -..- -
E .	M - -	U ..-	Question mark ..- -..
F ..-.	N -.	V ...-	Colon - - -...
G - -.	O - - -	W .- -	hyphen -....-
H	P .- -.	X -..-	

CREATIVE THINKING

Time: 120 seconds
Focus: Logic skills

First and last

Here are the first and last lines of a short story. Your task is to fill in the gap with a completely coherent story. Give yourself exactly a minute to tell the story out loud to yourself (or a friend) finishing with the last line exactly as your time runs out. Don't think about it too long. Plunge straight in and let your imagination race as you move towards the climax.

'Once upon a time, there was a magic fish that swam merrily through the sparkling green waters of the western ocean …

… And so the man vowed he would always remember to sow his corn in the field under the hill from now on.'

TIP: Keep the story flowing. Don't worry about trying to work out the entire story before you say each phrase. Just go where your imagination takes you as freely as possible. When you reread your story, give yourself marks for originality and how well you got your imagination and senses involved.

PART 2

SKILL DEVELOPING

Time: 15 minutes

As in the first session, your next task is to practise your chosen skill for 15 minutes.

Music test

Try and work out what these famous tunes are from the sequence of notes alone. If you have access to a musical instrument, play the first two notes only. Work the remaining notes out by humming them to yourself:

1. CEGACAGFG
2. AGEECCDC
3. GGAGCB–GGAGDC
4. What are the next two notes in this sequence:
   GGAGCB–GGAGDC–GG?

TIP: Again, if you can't guess the tune quickly, look up the answer on page 335 and then work through the list of notes given one by one, humming the tune to yourself. Don't sing the words, sing the note given, trying to hear its pitch. Practise this again and again for 15 minutes until you get the notes perfectly in your head.

PART 3

MIND MAPPING EXERCISE

Time: 15 minutes

Many people consider the advancement of age to be a negative experience, associating it with all sorts of terrible images such as walking sticks, dementia, lack of independence, loss of looks, isolation, boredom and even death! This is incredibly sad since growing older is an opportunity for growth and freedom and is a positive experience to be relished. We have only come to think of growing older in such negative terms fairly recently – consider all of the positive words there are for respected elders in society, such as guru, oracle, sensei, leader, matriarch, patriarch, master ... We have forgotten that age brings wisdom, experience and contentment. Of all things to forget, this is the most dangerous: if we anticipate a negative future for ourselves, it is far more likely to become a reality. Conversely, if you expect your life to keep getting better and better then in all likelihood it will.

Spend the next 15 minutes drawing a Mind Map (see page 57) to help you define a wholly positive experience of growing older. Start your Mind Map with a positive central image, for example a huge sun or a picture of a smiling, active person (you!). Label one of your branches 'definition' and expand on new positive labels for what you expect to experience, such as 'knowledge', 'leader', or 'confidence'. When you have explored this main branch, add another to your central image, this time relating to where you would like life to take you, such as 'goals', and fully explore this branch too. Keep adding new main branches and exploring them with sub-branches until the 15 minutes is up.

PART 4

MENTAL CUSHION: RELAXATION

Time: 15 minutes

Find a comfortable space where you won't be disturbed and spend 15 minutes practising the relaxation technique on page 102.

Sharpen up – DAY 4

Total time: 60 minutes

PART 1

BRAIN PRIMER

Time: 15 minutes (including time for checking answers)

MEMORY TONER AND MEMORY BUILDING

Time: 180 seconds
Focus: Short-term and long-term memory

True minds

For thousands of years, people used to learn poetry by heart. The bards of Ancient Greece and Ireland, and the troubadours of Medieval Europe, knew poems thousands of lines long to entertain audiences, and to pass on stories from generation to generation. It is well worth learning shorter poems, both for the tremendous exercise it gives to the memory and the sheer pleasure of having these wonderful words at your beck and call. Learn the first six lines of this famous sonnet by William Shakespeare in this session:

> Let me not to the marriage of true minds
> Admit impediments. Love is not love
> Which alters when it alteration finds,

Or bends with the remover to remove:
O no! it is an ever-fixed mark,
That looks on tempests and is never shaken;
[It is the star to every wandering bark,
Whose worth's unknown, although his height be taken.
Love's not Time's fool, though rosy lips and cheeks
Within his bending sickle's compass come:
Love alters not with his brief hours and weeks,
But bears it out even to the edge of doom.
If this be error and upon me proved,
I never writ, nor no man ever loved.]
William Shakespeare

TIP: The secret is to break the words into manageable chunks or phrases. Then:

1. Create a bold picture in your head to sum up each chunk. For example, for the phrase, 'Let me not to the marriage of true minds admit impediments' you might think of two heads going up the aisle to be married, then the church warden firmly barring an 'impediment', usually at the door.

2. Repeat the words in the chunk out loud rapidly, visualizing them until they become automatic.

WORD POWER

Time: 4 minutes
Focus: Language

In other words

It's easy to get by using the same old words every day – words that only convey part of what you really mean. For example, you could describe the hotel where you stayed on holiday as 'nice'. How much more informative it would be for your listeners if you described it as 'enchanting', 'beautiful', 'sleek', 'characterful' or 'lively'. Developing your ability to find just the right word is tremendous exercise for your brain – and will make your conversation more interesting, too. It's well worth getting a simple synonym dictionary or thesaurus. You can practise this every day. Just pick two words at random from the dictionary, close the book, see how many synonyms you can think of, then check your list against the dictionary. If you keep doing exercises like this then your vocabulary will increase indefinitely.

Here's a list of words to get you started. Your task is to find as many alternative words with similar meaning (synonyms) as you can within the time limit. Jot them down on paper.

abrupt	alarm
advance	big
deadly	hard
nice	appetizing
wet	brilliant
small	cool

LOGIC BOOSTER

Time: 120 seconds
Focus: Logic skills

Cruel Christmas
Solve this mystery
One snowy night in December, Inspector Courvoisier is hurrying home past the house of Monsieur Hubert. As he buttons up his collar against the heavily falling snow, he mutters ruefully about the lack of criminal activity in the village for him to investigate. Suddenly, he hears the unmistakable crackle of a single gunshot ring out from Hubert's house. Instantly, Courvoisier bursts into action, like a greyhound from a trap, racing up the path across the virgin snow. Within less than a minute, he reaches the front door to find Monsieur Hubert standing just inside in a state of shock. 'Oh my God!' moans Hubert as Courvoisier peers past him. Stretched out across the far side of the hall floor lies the body of Madame Hubert – a smoking gun in her limp hand and a vast pool of congealed blood staining the boards. 'I couldn't stop her!' Hubert whimpers, 'I just couldn't stop her. I was coming in from the village when I saw her with the gun. I was about to cry out when she pulled the trigger! It was horrible, horrible!' 'I see,' says Courvoisier. 'Would you mind taking two steps to the left.' Baffled, Hubert does as he is told. Courvoisier stares at the blank floor then nods. 'As I thought … Monsieur Hubert, you have lied to me. The shot I

heard was not the one which killed your wife. I am arresting you on suspicion of the murder of Madame Hubert.'

1. How does Courvoisier know Hubert was lying? What confirms it.

2. How does Courvoisier know that Madame Hubert was not killed by the shot he just heard?

3. What evidence is Courvoisier looking for when he asks Hubert to take two steps to the left? What does it prove?

ANALYTIC POWER

Time: 60 seconds
Focus: Logic skills

Morse code
Here's another coded message in Morse for you to work out (see page 116 for the key):

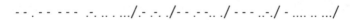

CREATIVE THINKING

Time: 120 seconds
Focus: Logic skills

First and last
Here are the first and last lines of a short story. Your task, as in Session three, is to fill in the gap with a completely coherent story. Give yourself exactly a minute to tell the story out loud to yourself, finishing with the last line exactly as your time

runs out. This time, though, record your story (on mobile phone, movie camera, computer, MP3 player or tape). Again, don't think about it too long. Plunge straight in and let your imagination race as you move towards the climax.

'Once upon a time, there was a big city where everyone wanted to be famous …

… And so the mouse said, 'Hey Nonny!' and scurried off beneath the floorboards.'

TIP: Again, keep the story flowing. Don't worry about trying to work out the entire story before you say each phrase. Just go where your imagination takes you as freely as possible.

PART 2

SKILL DEVELOPING

Time: 15 minutes

As in the previous sessions, your next task is to practise your chosen skill for 15 minutes.

PART 3

BEAT MEMORY BLOCKS

Time: 15 minutes

If there is one thing that everyone wants to avoid it is not being able to recall something when you know you know the answer – that feeling of it being on the tip of your tongue. The brain-stretching sessions in this book are designed to help prevent these kinds of memory blocks since the more you challenge your mind the stronger it becomes. In general, try to make a regular habit of revisiting old memories. This will improve your ability to recall information and events and help keep them fresh in your memory.

For this exercise, spend 15 minutes trying to remember your first day at secondary school in as much detail as possible. Remember the sights, the sounds, the smells. What happened? Who was there? How did you feel? Remember the names of as many people in your class and as many teachers as you can. What did they look like? Who was friends with who? Draw a Mind Map (see page 57) to help you explore your memories.

TIPS: Remembering names There'll be some names of classmates you remember easily, particularly if you were good friends with them. The names that are harder to recall, for example fellow students you didn't know very well, will be the ones that really exercise your brain. These names will often come back straightaway if you get the initial letter. Start by working slowly through the alphabet, experimenting with each letter. If one letter begins to sound right, say it out loud. Normally, the right name or word will eventually spring to mind.

Free association Psychologists often use free association of ideas to help build up a picture of people's unconscious minds. The idea is that the links are made before your conscious mind has the chance to censor them. It can also be a useful way of retrieving names, words and other facts when you have a mental block. Just relax and allow your mind to free associate around the vague idea. Explore any possible avenues, however irrelevant they seem. If you know the person played football, for instance, and can't remember the name, free associate around the topic of school football, remembering all that it meant to you. Very often you will find an unexpected link crops up and gives you the answer.

Forget about it Memories can be elusive as butterflies. Sometimes the sheer effort involved in beating a memory block appears to push the memory further away. The problem is that the enforced concentration forces your thoughts down one particular path, and prevents you connecting with the right associations. The answer is to go and do something completely different to distract yourself. Try getting up to make a cup of tea, going outside for a few minutes to get some fresh air, or simply do the washing up. By allowing your mind to wander, you often find the memory suddenly resurfaces effortlessly. Some people call this the 'law of reversed effort'.

PART 4

MENTAL CUSHION: RELAXATION

Time: 15 minutes

Find a comfortable space where you won't be disturbed and spend 15 minutes practising the relaxation technique on page 102.

Sharpen up – DAY 5

Total time: 60 minutes

PART 1

BRAIN PRIMER

Time: 15 minutes (including time for checking answers)

MEMORY TONER AND MEMORY BUILDING

Time: 180 seconds
Focus: Short-term and long-term memory

True minds
Start this session by learning a further six lines from the William Shakespeare sonnet:

[Let me not to the marriage of true minds
Admit impediments. Love is not love
Which alters when it alteration finds,
Or bends with the remover to remove:
O no! it is an ever-fixed mark,
That looks on tempests and is never shaken;]
It is the star to every wandering bark,
Whose worth's unknown, although his height be taken.
Love's not Time's fool, though rosy lips and cheeks
Within his bending sickle's compass come:

Love alters not with his brief hours and weeks,
But bears it out even to the edge of doom.
[If this be error and upon me proved,
I never writ, nor no man ever loved.]
William Shakespeare

TIP: As before, the secret is to break the words into manageable chunks or phrases. Create a bold picture in your head to sum up each chunk and repeat the words in the chunk out loud rapidly until they become automatic.

WORD POWER

Time: 180 seconds
Focus: Language

Word teaser ...
Try to think of as many synonyms as possible for each of the following words.

attitude	worry
awkward	rough
revolting	idiot
pleasant	fun
good	pretty
colourful	warm

TIP: This time, allow no more than 15 seconds per word before moving on to the next.

LOGIC BOOSTER

Time: 120 seconds
Focus: Logic skills

The runaway pony

Solve this mystery:

Inspector Courvoisier was enjoying a well earned holiday in the Camargue. It was a crisp spring morning and he could hear the birds chattering in the trees as he strolled down the country road. All of a sudden he heard a clatter of hooves behind him. He turned and saw a small, grey riderless pony galloping towards him, the reins trailing dangerously close to its legs and the stirrups flapping in the air. When the pony saw him it checked its pace and Courvoisier took the opportunity to grab the reins and bring it to a complete halt. 'Now to find your owner', he said, smoothing out its knotted forelock in an attempt to soothe it. Courvoisier wasn't really a horse person. However, he'd read somewhere that this could help calm a nervous mount. Courvoisier loosened the girth on the cracked saddle and started walking back in the direction the pony had come, keeping it on the inside of the road to shield it from any oncoming traffic. Perhaps he would come across the unseated owner.

A few minutes later a well dressed, stockily built young lady came running up the road, clearly out of breath and in some distress. 'Minette! Thank goodness I've found you!', she cried. 'Come, come you naughty animal, let's get you home.' Clearly ecstatic and thanking Courvoisier profusely, the young lady took the reins from him, leapt up on to Minette and dug her heels in to leave. At that precise moment a young boy came running down the lane. 'Stop her, stop her!' he shouted, 'That's my pony! She's working for a thief!' Courvoisier took the reins again. 'Don't be ridiculous!' the young lady said. 'How could a boy like that afford a pony like mine?' Courvoisier looked at the boy who by this time had reached the pony and was looking it up and down. 'Of course Mademoiselle,' he replied. 'Could you step down for a moment and we'll sort this out properly. I am Inspector Courvoisier and will see that this young boy is disciplined.' Pacified the lady dismounted next to Courvoisier. 'Now,' said Courvoisier turning to the boy, 'here is your pony. I hope you are feeling well enough to ride him. Mademoiselle, would you like to come with me? I am arresting you on suspicion of theft.'

1. What is it about the pony that doesn't match with the young lady's account?
2. How does the young lady's treatment of the pony prove she is not familiar with it?
3. What is it about the boy's manner that convinces Courvoisier it belongs to him?

ANALYTIC POWER

Time: 120 seconds
Focus: Logic skills

Morse code
Here's another coded message for you to work out in Morse:

.- -. .- .- - .... .. -. - -./... .../.- -. - - - ... . -... .-.. .

CREATIVE THINKING

Time: 120 seconds
Focus: Logic skills

First and last

Here are the first and last lines of a short story. Your task, as in the session yesterday, is to fill in the gap with a completely coherent story. As before, give yourself exactly a minute to tell the story out loud to yourself, finishing with the last line exactly as your time runs out. Record your story again (on mobile phone, movie camera, computer, MP3 player or tape) – you will be surprised how much easier it is to make your story hang together today. Again, don't think about it too long. Plunge straight in and let your imagination race as you move towards the climax.

'"I've had enough," said George, tearing off his wig. This time they could tell he really meant it …

… and the puffins scurried back into their burrows.'

TIP: Keep the story flowing. Don't worry about trying to work out the entire story before you say each phrase. Just go where your imagination takes you as freely as possible.

PART 2

SKILL DEVELOPING

Time: 15 minutes
As in the previous sessions, your next task is to practise your chosen skill for 15 minutes.

PART 3

MEMORY AND UNDERSTANDING

Time: 15 minutes (including time for checking answers)
The things we find hardest to remember are those that have no meaning for us. Establishing meaning is the key to remembering things. Sometimes, this meaning can be purely personal and emotional. For example, you would certainly remember when a person important to you sends you a huge bunch of flowers. Understanding is another important way of giving meaning. If you understand the things you see, or hear or read, there is a much better chance you will remember them.

Try these exercises in finding logic and meaning. Here is a list of words.

joy	cry
once	into
lark	girlfriend
woody	my
spiralling	nearby

of	wandering
my	in
see	a
the	the
moment	with
sheer	to
and	was
Paula	village
lane	downs
the	when
whooping	I
stopped	almost
the	I
a	over
saw	heart
enchanting	with
slowly	down
the	

Start off by spending 3 minutes to try to remember all the words. Use the quick-win memory technique that you think would work best. Cover up the book and write down as many of the words as you can. How did you do?

If you didn't get them all go back to the list again. Try to think about imposing some meaning on the words – they actually come from a broken sentence. Give yourself 1 minute to rearrange the words to form a complete sentence and then a further 3 to memorize the sentence. It doesn't matter if it isn't the same as the original; the idea is for you to come up with a version you can remember.

For example, 'a lark was spiralling nearby when I saw ...' Arrange the words into a meaningful sentence and you will find that you can remember them all easily. Making sense of the words in this way means they stick in your memory.

Now try this. Here is a random collection of 15 images. Using the same principles as above, give yourself 3 minutes to remember them all.

TIP: Arrange the images into a story board for a film.

PART 4

MENTAL CUSHION: RELAXATION

Time: 15 minutes

Find a comfortable space where you won't be disturbed and spend 15 minutes practising the relaxation technique on page 102.

Sharpen up – DAY 6

Total time: 60 minutes

CREATIVE EXPANSION

There is only one part to this session, and you will need to set aside a block of one hour to complete it uninterrupted. This time the aim is to push your creativity to new heights, developing the techniques you started in earlier sessions. Keep your creative juices flowing and you will keep your brain fit and agile.

Creativity depends on a number of different qualities:

Fluency – the speed and ease with which your brain bursts with all kinds of clever and original ideas.

Flexibility – your ability to see things from a new angle – turn a problem upside down, back to front and inside out to come at it afresh.

Originality – your ability to build your own unique ideas from scratch.

On the second day of this programme you had to find as many different uses as possible for a chocolate button. Today you're going to do a similar exercise only this time with a satellite dish. Below is a list of 30 random words. Your task is to find as many uses for a satellite dish connected to each word as you can. Once again, the key to this exercise is thinking outside the box and letting your imagination run riot – be as ridiculous and extravagant as you like!

Remember that your imagination will work best for you if you use:

Exaggeration The more exaggerated you make things, the more memorable they are – and the more they lead you in interesting directions. Your brain likes things big and lively.

Humour In the same way, making things totally ridiculous and outrageous helps make things more memorable and leads you in great, whacky directions.

Senses Your new input comes in through your senses – sight, touch, hearing, smell and taste. All of them can trigger memories – and new ideas. Try engaging your senses one by one. Imagine what smells might be linked to it, what tastes. And you'll find yourself wandering off down some interesting new pathways.

Colour Colours too have strong associations. Add in some vivid colours and it's surprising where your imagination will take you.

Pattern Your brain always looks for patterns and thinking of patterns can remind you of some completely new connections. What patterns could be made by satellite dishes and apples, for instance?

Rhythm and movement can take you in yet more directions.

Image Think of visual links to your subject and it can open up a flood of new associations and ideas.

1. Potato	11. Nuclear bomb	21. Holly
2. Bicycle	12. Tree	22. Christmas
3. Opera	13. Apple	23. Rabbit
4. Spaceship	14. Theatre	24. Golf
5. Umbrella	15. Cabinet	25. Camping
6. Knife	16. Hair	26. Rain
7. Fly	17. Flag	27. Swimming
8. Button	18. Weapon	28. Underwear
9. Butterfly	19. Shark	29. Church organ
10. Bandage	20. Diamond	30. Bowling

TIP: The best quick-win technique for this exercise is a Mind Map (see page 57). When you draw yours, make sure you do it in the following stages:

1. Draw a quick Mind Map with the satellite dish at the centre and brainstorm as many ideas, branches and colours as you can at high speed. Allow yourself 15 minutes.
2. Give yourself a 10-minute break – get up and do something completely different.
3. Return to your Mind Map and add any new ideas you've had.
4. Explore your Mind Map for another 15 minutes to find any new connections.
5. Connect elements by codes, colours and arrows.
6. Identify new connections.
7. Take a 10-minute break.
8. Return to your Mind Map for another 5 minutes, adding new ideas to each of the branches. Keep looking for new connections.

Sharpen up – DAY 7

Total time: 60 minutes

Today is a day of self-assessment and looking at the progress you have made. You should already be feeling sharper and more mentally agile and, if you keep building on this with The 7-Week Stay Sharp Plan in Chapter 8, you should soon become as mentally fit as someone ten years younger than you. The 7-Week Stay Sharp Plan isn't as intensive as The 7-Day Get Sharp Plan: you only need to set aside time one day a week for seven weeks.

PART 1

SELF-ASSESSMENT: YOUR PROGRESS

Time: 15 minutes

Revisit the 7-Minute Mind Makeover on page 4 and run through it again as quickly and perfectly as you can – can you do it in less time than 7 minutes? Assess your progress as honestly as you can and try to spot areas where you aren't quite as strong as you are in others. Make a note of these as The 7-Week Stay Sharp Plan in Chapter 8 will help you build on them.

PART 2

SELF-ASSESSMENT: WORD POWER

Time: 30 minutes

At the beginning of the last century, psychologists observed that there was a direct correlation between the size and strength of a person's vocabulary and a person's ability to succeed and achieve in life. In other words, people who harness the power of language give themselves the freedom and power to express themselves, wield influence and inspire others. Continue to expand your vocabulary throughout your life and you will continue to expand your horizons.

A simple way to get a rough idea of your vocabulary is to choose a page of a medium-grade dictionary at random, count the number of words you know the meaning of and then multiply your total by the number of pages. Here is a slightly more reliable guide. Count how many words you know in each level, using a dictionary to help you check the meaning of each:

Level 1

daily	manual
pattern	terminate
memorial	humdrum
contraband	harpoon
beverage	hardship
fatigue	vivacious

reign   distinct
expedition   purchase
alter   barometer
impulsive   excavate
report   abandon
jangle   chaos
cardinal   binoculars
demolish   stroke
waste   graph
shuttle   abroad
festival   limit
laboratory   matinee
horizon   parallel
rate   ballot

Level 2

laconic   territory
maelstrom   diverge
timbre   ecology
porous   prolixity
hybrid   lore
phantasm   restive
impunity   niche
redolent   facet
biography   domicile
interpose   actuate
decarbonize   cosmopolitan
lateral   rampant
paragon   vellum

muezzin

stertorous

bravura

comber

taboo

gouache

yeoman

iconoclast

linden

hieroglyphic

voodoo

resurgent

maxilla

Level 3

pedicular

geodesic

champlevé

deadlight

samphire

oblate

vavasor

Chamfer

jokul

maud

spandrel

laches

giaour

ukase

enchiridion

imprest

lapidate

nadir

eschatology

satrap

In the first two levels, each word you know suggests that you know about 300 other words.

Your score:

> If you get 20 right at level 1, it suggests you know about 6,000–10,000 words.
>
> If you get all 40 right in level 1, it suggests that you know at least 12,000 words.
>
> If you get 20 right at level 2, it suggests that you know at least 18,000 words.
>
> If you know all 40 at level 2, it suggests you know at least 24,000 words.
>
> If you know more than 10 at level 3, it suggests you know more than 30,000 words.

Word teaser ...

Select 10 words you know from the first level, 5 from the second and 5 from the third and think of as many synonyms as possible for each. Allow yourself no more than 15 seconds per word or 5 minutes in total.

PART 3

MENTAL CUSHION: RELAXATION

Time: 15 minutes

Find a comfortable space where you won't be disturbed and spend 15 minutes practising the relaxation technique on page 102.

PART TWO

Chapter 5

Strong body, strong mind

'I am long on ideas, but short on time.
I expect to live to be only about 100.'

Thomas Alva Edison

Now you have completed The 7-Day Get Sharp Plan, your brain should be buzzing with new techniques and energy! What else can you do to keep it in peak condition? Many people are now realizing that keeping your body strong and fit keeps your mind strong and fit too.

BODY AND MIND

In the past it was assumed that intellectual performance and physical fitness were two entirely different things. Some people were said to be all brawn and no brain. Others were all brain and no brawn. Now research is beginning to show what some people have always argued: that there is no separating mind and body. Your brain is a part of your body and your physical health has a profound effect on your mental health – and vice versa.

Over the last few decades great strides have been made in our physical health and nowadays people in the developed world are undoubtedly living longer than ever before. A century ago, a baby girl in Australia could expect to live no more than 58 years on average. Now she can expect to live to 83 on average, a shift of a massive 25 years. And the fact that the average has shifted this much means that a great many Australian women are living beyond the age of 83.

It's nothing new for people to live well beyond 83, of course. History is full of famous examples of centenarians. What's changed is that a century ago, an 83-year lifespan was a rarity. Now it is the norm. A similar thing has been happening in the fitness levels of older people. A century ago, it was rare for old people to be fit and healthy. Now it is the norm.

What's more, some of these over-60s are so fit that there is now a Veterans' Olympics in which veterans compete to a very high standard. Any slight drop in their physical performance is often more than matched by the benefits of a lifetime's experience. Sixty-four-year-old UK squash player Mike Thurgur is one such inspiring example: in a recent charity event he was on court for 15 hours non-stop, taking on all comers – including many national-level players a third his age – and beat them all. Equally impressive is the astronaut John Glenn: he coped with the rigours of space travel at the age of 77.

LONG LIFE, GOOD HEALTH

The average age of people around the world is going up and up. Already, 1 in 10 are over 60. The United Nations estimate that by 2050, 1 in 5 will be. As this 'greying' of humanity gathers pace, more and more of us will be over 80, and many will even be over 100.

This is a phenomenal achievement. Barely a century ago, very few people ever had the chance to reach their 80s and beyond. All too many were cut down in their prime by disease and hardship. In 1900, 99 in every 100 people would die before they even reached 60. Only 1 in 100 would live long enough to collect a pension. The rare privilege of living out anywhere near the full human lifespan was reserved for a tiny élite. Now, thanks to better diet, steady improvements in public health and the benefits of modern medicine, most us can expect to live until our 90s and beyond. In the West, life expectancy is going up year by year. Every American baby born in the year 2004 can expect to live to the age of 77.9 years on average. White girls can expect to live to nearly 81.

What's more, people are not just living longer – they are staying healthy too. Amazingly, in the wealthier parts of the world, where the population has grown oldest, spending on health and social care on the very old has gone *down*. Over the past century, modern medicine, better sanitation and an improved diet have helped people live much longer *and healthier* lives.

Could we live forever?

Some scientists believe that we will soon expect to live a lot longer than 80 or 90. Tun Dr Ling is one of them. Tun Dr Ling is a qualified medical doctor who is carrying out extraordinary research in the field of ageing. He believes that we are close to approaching a time when we could dramatically increase our life spans by several hundred years.

Rather than basing his research on cryogenics (freezing people until such time as there is enough medical knowledge to keep them alive), it is based on revolutionary new advances in medicine that enable a person's organs to be grown from that person's own cells. The significance of this is that the body receiving the organs won't reject them since they are made from the same DNA. Scientists have already succeeded in creating a new bladder in this way and they are now carrying out the same research on 23 other major body organs, including the liver, spleen and heart. He and the other scientists working in this field believe that once they crack growing all the major organs in the body we could all live as long as 350 years!

THE BRAIN BENEFITS OF EXERCISE

The physical benefits of exercise have been known about for a long time. In China, there is even a national programme of Tai Chi to encourage national health and ease pressure on the health system. Now, research is showing that your state of mind can influence your physical health, and physical health can influence brain health. On the one hand, depression and stress have been shown to suppress the body's immune system and make people more prone to infections and a variety of other illnesses. On the other, physical exercise has been shown to alleviate depression.

A recent study of 156 patients between 50 and 77 suffering major depression divided them into three groups. One group was treated with medication, another was encouraged to exercise and the third was given both medication and exercise. The exercise group spent 30 minutes three times a week either riding a stationary bicycle, walking or jogging. To the surprise of the researchers, all three groups showed improvement in their depression, indicating that exercise is just as effective in treating depression as medication.

Physical exercise certainly helps you live better and more healthily, and now research has shown a direct connection between brain ageing and mental fitness. A major study in Quebec of 5,000 men and women over 65 showed that those who exercised regularly were less likely to show decline in their mental performance or develop Alzheimer's and similar diseases. Moreover, the more a person exercised, particularly women, the greater the benefits. Those who did no exercise at all were twice as likely to develop Alzheimer's as those who exercised at least three times a week. Even light exercise cut the risk of Alzheimer's significantly.

Another study looked at the benefits of simply walking regularly. Researchers in San Francisco led by Kristine

Yaffe followed a group of 6,000 women over eight years, monitoring their memory and other mental functions in comparison to their level of activity. Over the period of the study, those who walked least showed 50 per cent more deterioration than those who walked most. What's more, Yaffe discovered that you can experience the benefits whatever your level of mental fitness. She found that every little helps. For every extra mile a woman walked a week, there was a 13 per cent less chance of cognitive decline.

BRAIN FACTS

Exercising in the mind

An extraordinary recent study at the Cleveland Clinic in the USA showed that just as muscle exercise can improve brain fitness, your mind might be able to strengthen your muscles just by thinking about it. For 12 weeks, the clinic's Dr Vinoth Ranganathan got 30 healthy young adults to think regularly about moving either a little finger or an elbow, without actually moving them. Astonishingly, those who thought about moving a little finger found it over a third stronger after three months, while those who thought about moving an elbow found it 13 per cent stronger. Ranganathan believed that the strength gains came because the brain learned how to signal the muscle to contract better, rather than the muscle actually gaining in bulk.

The theory is that exercise improves blood circulation. Improved circulation increases the supply of oxygen and glucose to the brain, giving it extra energy as well as all the other chemicals it needs. It also helps clear away waste products more efficiently. This is why a brisk walk quite literally 'clears your head'.

Getting started

Now you can see the brain benefits of exercise, are you raring to go? Before you start, it's always useful to consult your doctor about starting a fitness programme. They will probably be delighted to hear about your ideas!

Something else to do before you begin is to consider the four main areas of physical fitness:

1. poise
2. aerobic training
3. flexibility
4. strength

POISE

A definition of poise is 'a graceful and elegant bearing'. If you are perfectly poised, your body is perfectly balanced, with all the muscles, joints and organs in the proper place, and there is a natural flow of energy throughout your bodily systems. So far, so good, except what does this have to do with exercise? Put simply, if you exercise with poise – that is, with balance and composure – it can really enhance all the benefits of exercise and radically reduce the risk of injury or strain, something that becomes especially important as you grow older.

The value of poise was realized primarily through the work of Matthias Alexander, who pioneered the 'Alexander Technique' of movement and posture in the last century. Information on the Alexander Technique is widely available, if you would like to find out more. In the meantime, why not do a quick 'poise check'?

Wherever you are, whatever you are doing, ask yourself the following questions:

1. Am I slouching?
2. Am I slumping forward or pulling my neck back?
3. Am I stiffening or raising my shoulders?
4. Am I locking any joints?
5. Am I leaning back with my hips and the small of my back forward?
6. Am I breathing in a light, shallow way or deeply and fully?

If you find your posture is in need of improvement, just relax for a moment, pause and then bring yourself back into alignment with what is known as 'Alexander's Primary Control posture':

1. Make sure your neck is relaxed and free.
2. Straighten your head.
3. Adjust your posture – your back should be open and wide.
4. Focus on reducing any areas of tension in your breathing or your body.

One way to improve your poise is to become aware of it at intervals throughout the day. Take a moment now and then to check your poise and bring yourself back into alignment, and soon you will find yourself adopting a more balanced posture naturally.

If you need some inspiration, why not put some pictures of people or animals with pose, such as dancers or big cats, around your home or office? Or why not take up a new hobby? Activities that help to develop poise include:

1. yoga
2. Alexander technique
3. dance
4. Tai Chi and Chi Kung
5. Aikido and other martial arts

AEROBIC TRAINING

'Aerobic' exercise is any exercise that stimulates heart and lung activity for long enough to produce beneficial changes in your body. Walking, running, cycling and swimming are all examples of aerobic exercise. They all increase the ability of your body to utilize oxygen – and that has a whole range of benefits for your brain as well as your body. Studies at the Salk Institute have shown that running can boost the survival of brain cells in mice that have diseases similar to Alzheimer's and actually stimulate cell growth in the human brain.

To become and stay aerobically fit you need to exercise just four times a week for a minimum of 30 minutes a time. Each exercise session should consist of:

- **a 5-minute warm-up**
- **20 minutes of exercise**
- **a 5-minute cool-down and stretch**

Walking, dancing, swimming and running are simple forms of exercise you might like to try out and are easy ways of incorporating your aerobic training into your daily life. The 7-Week Stay Sharp Plan will help you build in time for exercise.

For now, the key is to start slowly and to be gentle with yourself. You will soon be feeling both mental and physical benefits! Research conducted by Dr James Blumathal at Duke University Medical Center showed that just half-an-hour of aerobic activity three times a week boosted memory and mental fitness in people of all ages – most significantly in the middle-aged and elderly. Moreover, the improvement was both immediate and long-lasting – even better!

FLEXIBILITY

Flexibility refers to the freedom and ease with which your body's joints move. When your body is flexible, oxygen can flow more freely, including to your brain. This helps boost your mental fitness too. Simply stretching in all directions is one of the best flexibility exercises there is and one that you can do quickly and easily every day.

The exercise suggestions to help your poise will also help with flexibility, as will the warm-up and cool-down periods of your aerobic exercise.

STRENGTH

Strength training is also a vital part of physical fitness. It strengthens your muscles, tones your body, makes you feel good and helps you to maintain health and all-round fitness.

At Tufts University in the United States, 86–96-year-old nursing-home residents undertook an eight-week weight-training programme which resulted in dramatic increases in strength and improvements in balance. Continued weight training with either free weights or machines improved arthritis, increased bone density and even moderated insulin insensitivity in Type 2 diabetics.

To increase muscle fitness, you need to exercise four times each week for between 20 and 60 minutes, depending on the muscles being worked. You might like to exercise at home or join a class or a gym – there could be social benefits too! To find out what's available in your area, why not check out your local library or look on the Internet?

BRAIN FACTS

Brains and muscles

Brains and muscles are far more intimately connected than you might imagine. In the same way that neurons connect with each other in the brain, they connect directly to muscles. Motor neurons connect the brain to muscles to make them contract. Sensory neurons connect the muscles with the brain to provide them with feedback. The neurons make contact with the muscle across a fine gap called the 'neuromuscular junction'. What's interesting is that communication across this gap is carried by some of the same neurotransmitters that are used in the brain, including acetylcholine, the brain's memory and attention signaller, and dopamine, its reward signaller, both of which play a key role in brain ageing.

There is no doubt that muscle activity and brain function are actually deeply involved. Many masseurs testify, for instance, that deep massage can trigger the release of long-forgotten, highly emotional memories.

DOING IT ALL

There are several forms of exercise that develop poise, aerobic fitness, flexibility *and* strength, all together. What's more, these amazing all-round exercises can be enjoyable too! They are:

1. walking
2. running
3. swimming
4. dancing
5. rowing
6. Aikido and other martial arts

Whatever form of exercise you choose to take, make sure that it becomes part of your daily routine. In addition to age-proofing your brain, it will make you healthier, happy and more confident about your body.

Chapter 6

Feed your mind

Tell me what you eat, and I will tell you what you are.

Anthelme Brillat-Savarin,
18th-century French epicure and gastronome

Feed your body and you feed your mind too. Scientists are now realizing that diet plays a key part in brain fitness. Remarkable though it is, your brain is simply a tiny chemical processor, and it needs a steady supply of the right chemicals if it is to function well – and these chemicals, more than anything, come from the food you eat. Mental agility in later life has been linked to dietary deficiencies or excesses. It is important to feed your mind well – you could benefit both now and in the future.

BRAIN FUEL

Your brain needs energy in the form of glucose. It needs proteins for building and repairing neurons. It needs fats to protect them. And it needs vitamins and minerals to help make vital chemicals such as neurotransmitters. To get all these substances, you need the right balance of nutrients in your diet. Eat the right balance of foods and you may help protect your mental powers against decline both in the long and the short term.

When it comes to energy, your brain is the most demanding organ in your body. Although it is just 2 per cent or less of your body weight, it uses a fifth of your body's energy intake. This is why eating enough energy food is crucial for good brain function.

Energy in your food comes in the form of chemicals called carbohydrates, such as sugars and starches. Your brain can only use them in one form, glucose, meaning that the body has to convert most carbohydrates into glucose for your brain to use them. The glucose is delivered to the brain in the blood and absorbed through the blood-brain barrier (BBB).

Some sweet foods, such as fizzy drinks, sweets and many fast foods, contain sugars in simple forms that are very easily absorbed and quickly changed into glucose. You might think that this would be great for your brain, providing instant energy. Unfortunately, it is just *too* usable – a point that can be illustrated by something as seemingly plain as paper. Although paper is great for getting a fire started, it burns too quickly to give out a steady heat. In the same way, sugary foods are just too readily burned up to make good brain food if consumed in large quantities.

For a start, sugary foods are so easily converted by your body into glucose that there is a sudden rise in blood sugar levels. Your body quickly produces insulin in response to this sugar rush, in an effort to bring sugar levels down. The result is your blood sugar levels swing wildly from high to low. In the short term, this can cause dizziness, anxiety, headaches, thirst, confusion and tiredness.

A sugar rush can also bring on 'brain fog', where you are unable to think clearly because of the unbalanced blood sugar levels.

SWEET DAMAGE

In the long term, a diet with excess sugars can slow the activity of your brain down, as it adjusts to these continuous floods of blood sugar. Feed the body continually with a high-sugar diet and it adjusts by becoming less sensitive to insulin. Low insulin sensitivity means that body cells, especially brain cells, begin to starve themselves of sugar. Toronto professor Carol Greenwood showed that people with insulin resistance who were already slower learners got much worse after a sugary snack.

It seems the more you feed your brain with the wrong kind of fuel, the faster it burns out – and the worse it performs. High-sugar diets seem such bad news that some scientists have suggested that the best way to protect your brain against ageing is to restrict your calorie intake. The evidence seems to be that cutting calories cuts the damage done by free radicals. Free radicals play a key role in the ageing process by damaging cell membranes, proteins and DNA, the cells' master chemicals. Neurons are thought to be especially susceptible to free-radical damage.

A restricted calorie intake also puts your brain under mild stress, making it produce BDNFs (brain-derived neurotropic factors), which protect neurons. It is thus better equipped to deal with long-term deterioration and stress. Baltimore neuroscientist Mark Mattson discovered that animals kept on a calorie-reduced diet had more active brains because, apparently, they were looking for food.

While the idea of a calorie-restricted diet remains somewhat controversial, neuroscientists agree that most people can afford to cut down their carbohydrate intake. It is also makes sense to cut down on simple sugary food, especially refined sugar, and eat more complex carbohydrates, found in foods such as vegetables.

FAT HEADS

Fats are another source of energy in the diet. They are also useful building materials for the brain. In fact, one third of your brain is made of fat. Fats make great electrical insulation, and they play a key role in the myelin sheaths that coat nerves, just as electrical wires are coated in plastic.

There are two main kinds of dietary fats – saturated and unsaturated, depending on their chemical structure. Vegetable fats are mostly unsaturated and can be beneficial, since they are used to make essential hormones such as prostaglandins. Animal fats are mainly saturated and, in excess, have long been thought to contribute to heart disease and other diseases. They are now implicated in Alzheimer's, because they contribute to obesity, raised blood cholesterol and high blood pressure. Most experts agree that fats of all kinds should contribute no more than a third of your calorie intake.

FISH FOOD

In recent years, a lot of people have talked about how oily cold-water fish, such as herring, is the ultimate brain food. This means that all those fishy spoonfuls of cod liver oil we swallowed as children weren't in vain – our parents were right after all! Fish oil is rich in the fatty acid Omega 3, which is thought to have a wide range of benefits. Apart from being good for our physical health, including reducing the risk of heart attack and the joint pain associated with rheumatism, it is now widely believed to contribute to our mental health too.

Many scientists think Omega 3 is a vital brain food at both ends of our lives. Indeed, some scientists argue it is the key food in age-proofing your brain. A recent study of 4,000 older people in Chicago showed that among those who ate fish at least once a week, mental sharpness and memory declined 10 per cent more slowly. Among those who ate two fish meals a week, it was 13 per cent slower. The researchers likened it to knocking three to four years off your mental age.

Omega 3 is vital brain food partly because a form of Omega 3 called DHA (docosahexaenoic acid) makes up a significant portion of the membranes of neurons. It also encourages the production of BDNFs, which help promote new neuron growth and connections. And it plays a role in boosting the key neurotransmitters dopamine and serotonin. The decline of these is thought to contribute to brain ageing.

Brain food

Foods for neurotransmitters

Certain foods seem to be crucial for the brain to start making neurotransmitters. Any shortage of these precursors in the diet can lead to poor mental function. They include:

1. aspartic acid, used to make aspartate, found in peanuts, potatoes and eggs and grains
2. choline, used to make acetylcholine, found in eggs, liver and soya beans
3. glutamic acid, used to make glutamate, found in flour and potatoes
4. phenylalanine, used to make dopamine, found in beetroot, soya beans, almonds, eggs, meat and grains
5. tryptophan, used to make serotonin, found in eggs, lean meat, fish, bananas, peanuts, dates, yoghurt, milk and cheese
6. tyrosine, used to make noradrenalin, found in meat, fish and legumes

There are actually various Omega oils besides Omega 3, including Omega 6. Omega 6 is sometimes portrayed as the 'bad' Omega oil while Omega 3 is the 'good' one. Although one of Omega 3's key benefits is to reduce the damaging impact of Omega 6, it's not as simple as that. Omega 6, found in such foods as vegetable oils, eggs, poultry and cereals, helps to keep your skin healthy and helps your blood to clot properly.

What is needed is the right balance between Omega 3 and Omega 6. The argument is that our modern diet has become swamped in Omega 6 with the increased use of vegetable oils in cooking and processing, while at the same time being starved of Omega 3 as we eat less oily fish.

BRAIN FACTS

How we beat the apes with fish

Some scientists, such as Professor Michael Crawford, Head of the Institute of Brain Chemistry and Human Nutrition in London, believe that it was eating fish that helped Homo become Homo sapiens – in other words, it was fish that made us clever. Eating meat and vegetables, our brains could not develop that far, whatever their size. When early humans began to live by the sea and eat seafood, perhaps shellfish collected from pools, it gave such a boost to the connections between brain cells that their intellectual prowess came on in leaps and bounds.

THE DANGEROUS FATS

There is one kind of unsaturated fat which is really bad news: trans fat. Trans fats are found naturally in small quantities in meat and dairy products. These days the main source of trans fats in our diet is from plant oils made thicker by adding hydrogen, a process called 'hydrogenation'. Until recently, these hydrogenated fats were found in virtually every processed food in huge quantity. Unlike animal fats, they survive the high temperatures which allow such food to be made very quickly, they increase its water content, they extend its shelf life – and they are cheap.

Recently, however, research has shown that trans fats are more deeply implicated in heart disease than saturated fats, lowering the levels of the 'good' cholesterol (HDL) in the blood and raising the levels of the 'bad' cholesterol (LDL). Now scientists are finding evidence that trans fats can be bad for the brain too. It seems they push out good fats such as Omega 3, making neuron membranes thicker and more rigid, and consequently worse at receiving neurotransmitters.

Because of these problems, trans fats have been banned in the USA. They remain a key ingredient in bread and many other processed foods in Europe. Some food makers have moved to replace hydrogenated fats with palm oils, which may turn out to be just as harmful. It makes sense therefore to cut down on processed foods, baked products and factory-baked bread as much as possible if you want to avoid the damaging effects of these artificial oils.

THE THINKING AND FEELING NUTRIENTS

Vitamins are chemicals that in small quantities are vital for health. Deficiencies in any of them can be damaging. For the brain, a group called the B vitamins is particularly important. B vitamins are thought to lower levels of homocysteine, a blood protein linked to heart disease, as well as Alzheimer's and other types of dementia, while a kind of B vitamin called folic acid may also help prevent Alzheimer's, as it has a role in dealing with fatty acids in the brain.

The B vitamins are also sometimes dubbed 'the thinking and feeling nutrients' because they play such a vital role in nourishing the nervous system. There are at least ten groups of them and they work in keeping the communication between nerve cells up to speed. Many help form neurotransmitters.

Shortages of B vitamins are linked to a lot of brain-health problems. Prolonged B1 shortage can lead to psychosis and maybe lower intelligence. B3 supplements can help migraines and headaches, and have been used to treat schizophrenia. B5 is sometimes known as the 'anti-stress vitamin' because of its role in controlling adrenalin. It is also thought to boost memory.

The B vitamin that is exciting especial interest when it comes to brain-ageing is B12, which helps form the myelin sheath that insulates nerves. Various studies have shown that people with Alzheimer's typically have reduced B12 levels, while from the other end, other studies have shown that people with reduced B12 levels are more likely to develop the disease. The evidence is growing that B12 might protect you against Alzheimer's. It may also boost your memory.

As we get older, we can lose some of our ability to absorb B12 from food – particularly if we use antacids a lot or drink alcohol frequently. One in 200 elderly people lack the gastric secretions necessary to absorb B12 altogether. In such cases, a doctor may recommend B12 injections to make up the deficit. Some doctors also recommend that adults over 50 eat food fortified with extra B12.

For most people, though, dietary B12 is enough. Indeed, upping the B12 content of your diet can be enough to reverse lapses in memory and slight problems with co-ordination and balance. Sometimes, this just means eating plenty of fish, offal, pork and eggs. Because B12 needs folic acid to work well, it is also worth eating foods rich in folic acid such as bananas, oranges and lemons, green leafy vegetables and lentils.

Brain food

Sources of B vitamins

1. B1 (thiamine): wholegrain and enriched grain products like bread, rice, pasta, fortified cereals and pork
2. B5 (panthothenic acid): meat, poultry, fish, wholegrain cereals, legumes, vegetables and fruit
3. B6 (pyridoxine): chicken, fish, pork, liver, kidney, plus nuts and legumes
4. B12 (cyanocobalamin): eggs, meat, fish and poultry

5. Folic acid: green leafy vegetables, bananas, oranges and lemons, cantaloupe, strawberries and lentils

MINERAL POWER

Besides vitamins, a number of minerals are needed for brain health. Calcium, needed for healthy bones, also plays a vital part in nerve-signal transmission – as do potassium and sodium. Given that most people have too much sodium in their diets in the form of salt, you need to balance this with extra potassium (*for sources, see below*). Zinc is also important for brain function. You may be deficient in this if your diet is too rich in iron, or if you smoke, drink or are stressed. Other important elements needed in tiny quantities for brain fitness are manganese, copper and selenium.

Brain food

Sources of minerals

1. Magnesium: wholegrains, legumes, nuts, sesame seeds, dried figs
2. Potassium: apricots, avocados, bananas, melons, grapefruit, kiwi fruit, oranges, strawberries, prunes, potatoes, pulses, meat, fish
3. Calcium: fish with edible bones, sesame seeds
4. Zinc: oysters, red meat, peanuts, sunflower seeds
5. Selenium: meat and fish, Brazil nuts, avocados, lentils
6. Manganese: nuts, cereals, brown rice, pulses

7. Copper: offal, shellfish such as oysters, nuts and seeds, mushrooms, cocoa

CURRY ON THINKING

Recent studies by Greg Cole of UCLA suggests that curry might be as good for your brain as oily fish. Cole's team found that mice dosed with the Omega 3 oil ingredient DHA were at least partially protected against Alzheimer's. Then the team fed the mice exactly the same amount of curcumin, an ingredient of the curry spice turmeric, that an average person in India eats every day. They found it gave just as good protection against Alzheimer's as DHA.

Brain food

Water

Your body is composed of around 75 per cent water, and water is vital for the functioning of every part of it, including your brain. Drinking plenty of water will help your overall health and your mental health too. Two litres/eight glasses of water drunk at intervals throughout the day is ideal, combined with good physical activity.

EAT YOUR GREENS!

Age-old wisdom has always told us to eat our greens, and now research seems to be showing why. A 10-year study of over 13,000 American female nurses in their sixties showed that those who ate more vegetables showed markedly less decline over the years in a battery of tests of memory and learning. Indeed, the more vegetables they ate, the better they performed. Key vegetables were broccoli, cauliflower, lettuces and spinach.

RED, RED WINE!

Just recently a number of neuroscientists have been singing the praises of red wine, or rather a key ingredient of red wine called resveratrol. Italian scientist Alessandro Cellini found that fish given high doses of resveratrol lived 60 per cent longer, and when other fish died of old age at 12 weeks, these Methusaleh fish still had the mental agility of young fish. Resveratrol seemed to protect the fish's brain cells against age-related decline.

Similar studies show that resveratrol is an antioxidant, protecting cells by mopping up free radicals, while others show that it actually encourages nerve cells to regrow. One group of researchers even suggested that a glass or two of wine a day can increase neural connections sevenfold. It may even protect against Alzheimer's. That's got to be good news! Cheers!

Chapter 7

Kill stress, cure the mind

In times of stress, be bold and valiant.

Horace

The pace and pressures of modern society leaves many people in a state of permanent anxiety and stress. How many people have you spoken to in the last week who have complained about feeling stressed? Probably quite a few. Worrying can be addictive and once you get into the habit you can worry about anything and everything, whether it's your family, job, health, finances, the state of the country, the state of the world ... Once you get going the list can be endless! Unfortunately, as well as interfering with your ability to remember things, chronic levels of stress can prematurely age your brain. It is therefore absolutely vital that you are able to manage the levels of stress in your life and find ways to deal with what life throws at you in the most positive and constructive way possible. This chapter takes a look at the effects of stress on your body and mind and the steps you can take to keep it at bay.

All of us are born with an instinctive response to tricky situations – the stress response. Whenever we are faced with a dangerous situation, the brain instantly galvanizes the body into action. A rapid burst of nerve impulses to the appropriate muscles makes us duck, cover our heads, jump out of the way or whatever is most appropriate. And at the same time, the brain sends out an alarm signal to the adrenal glands on top of the kidneys. This triggers two hormones, adrenalin and noradrenalin, to immediately flood out from the adrenals and into the bloodstream. A third, cortisol, oozes out a little later.

READY FOR ACTION

What adrenalin and noradrenalin do is instantly prepare the body for emergencies. We can deal with many situations by standing to face the threat or by running away. This is why it is called the 'fight or flight' response. Together the hormones boost the supply of oxygen and energy in the body, delivering more glucose to the muscles and shutting down distracting body processes such as digestion.

Adrenalin and noradrenalin:
1. make your heart beat more quickly and strongly
2. boost the blood supply to your muscles
3. cut the blood supply to your skin, making you go pale

4. make you breathe more quickly and deeply to boost the oxygen supply to your muscles
5. make you sweat
6. make your pupils widen to help you see better

Cortisol:

1. prepares your body for the after-effects of danger (such as injury)
2. unlocks the energy of fat
3. mobilizes amino acids to help repair damaged cells
4. helps reduce pain, which is one reason why the pain of an injury can take a little while to kick in

This reaction can be life saving in dangerous situations. It can give you the superhuman power to beat off a wild dog attacking your child or to run away when you see a car about to explode. The problem is that most of the stressful situations in which we find ourselves don't require a superhuman physical reaction on this level. Although you may wish to run a mile when you have to stand up and give a speech, you need to stay put and deliver your words eloquently!

STRESS AND BRAIN-AGEING

The stress response can become a problem if it is always kicking in when there is no real danger, for example when you miss a train, your internet connection breaks down, or someone records over your favourite film. It can also interfere if you are the kind of person who worries about everything all the time. When this happens, the stress response hormones start working – and with nowhere to go, the result is chronic stress. It's this that you need to avoid.

Chronic stress can have many damaging effects on your body and in recent years it has become clear that it can also have a direct impact on the rate your brain ages. This seems to work through cortisol. Ageing makes brain cells in the hippocampus less responsive to cortisol and consequently less able to control the levels of stress hormones.

There is also increasing evidence that cortisol, and in particular glucocorticoid, can have a directly ageing effect on your brain. Stress and ageing seem to be two sides of the same dark coin: stress ages the brain, and the signs of chronic stress in the brain are often indistinguishable from those of ageing. In animal experiments, raised cortisol levels induced by stress seem to have the same damaging affect on the brain as ageing. Prolonged exposure to glucocorticoids also seems to reduce brain cells' ability to reroute connections to other brain cells or to make new ones. The problem is particularly acute in the hippocampus, the region of the brain linked with laying down memories. This probably accounts for why too much stress can interfere with your memory. At high levels, glucocorticoids can kill brain cells in experimental animals and it is thought that the same happens in humans.

This is why reducing the levels of stress in your life is an essential part of age-proofing your brain and protecting your memory.

A QUESTION OF BALANCE

Before you decide to spend the rest of your life lying comatose on a beach, don't! Believe it or not, a certain amount of stress in your daily life is in fact quite good for you: going to weddings, watching football matches or even meeting new people. Although they can all be highly stressful, it's these buzzes that help make life worth living. In the right doses, stress keeps you on your toes and helps to keep you focused and motivated. Stress can also toughen you up mentally and help you deal appropriately with tricky situations. Problems only emerge when you are under constant pressure and can never fully recover between stressful situations.

Research led by British scientist Steven Rose found that whereas long-term exposure to high cortisol levels damaged the hippocampus, the right amount could actually enhance learning and memory. Rose described how his research chicks were usually kept in pairs to avoid distressing them. If pairs reared together were suddenly separated, their blood corticosteroid level rose and they showed better retention and recall.

In recent years, some scientists have been interested in 'hormesis'. This is the idea that in small doses, 'stressors' such as poisons, radiation and heat can keep you alive longer. The theory is that when your body is exposed to these stressors, it overshoots in its repair work, with heat-shock proteins and DNA first-aid enzymes, and actually repairs cells damaged by ageing.

Researchers at Johns Hopkins University in Baltimore noticed a similar effect with 28,000 nuclear shipyard workers. They found death rates were 24 per cent *lower* than in a similar group of non-nuclear shipyard workers. Another researcher also found that radiologists lived longer than other doctors. All this suggests that exposure to low levels of stressors, such as poison and radiation, can extend life in the right doses. The difficulty of course is working out what stressors work best with humans, and in what doses. (Some researchers argue that the best might be low-level hunger – though that might not be a very popular option!)

What, therefore, can you do to balance stress in your life?

ACCENTUATE THE POSITIVE

One of the best ways to keep calm and focused is to look for the positive in every situation – to expect there to be a solution rather than a problem. If you have a tendency to view minor hiccoughs as disasters you will expose yourself to unnecessary stress. If you always exaggerate the severity of a problem, for example – 'If I miss that deadline, I'm not going to get paid, and if I don't get paid, how can I get the drains fixed, and if I can't get the drains fixed, how can I keep the house clean, and if the house isn't clean …' – then you will be using up valuable thinking power worrying about and prolonging the problem when you could actually be resolving it. Psychologists call this 'catastrophizing'.

Take this quiz to see if you are one of life's positive thinkers. Simply answer 'yes' or 'no' to the following questions:

1. I like myself.
2. I am worth cherishing.
3. I am good.
4. I see my strengths and weaknesses in perspective.

5. I am rarely critical of myself.
6. I have as much right to happiness as anyone.
7. I am as likely to find happiness as anyone.
8. If I ever fail, I can always try again.

Now try these:

1. I often make dramatic statements such as, 'No one ever asks me' or 'I always get it wrong.'
2. I usually see the limitations of my successes.
3. It's not worth doing anything if you don't complete it.
4. I can sometimes tell exactly what someone's thinking.
5. I often think life isn't fair.
6. I often think people are being critical.

Ideally you should have answered 'yes' to most of the first set of questions and 'no' to the second. If, however, you answered 'no' to most of the first set of questions and 'yes' to most of the second set, you need to take steps to break your negative habits. How can you change? You could start with these basic ideas:

- **Think of a number of very simple tasks you can do each day – wipe the bathroom mirror, empty the rubbish bin, for example – and make a mental note to praise yourself when you do them. Forget those you failed to do. Keep the tasks very easy at first – the easier the better.**
- **Just before you go to bed, write down or make a mental note of three good things that happened during the day.**

- Avoid speculating about people's motives; respond only to what they do and say.

KEEP SMILING

Another quick-win way to reduce stress is simply to feel happy. Scientists have already discovered that a positive attitude can cut in half the chances of older men suffering heart disease – and even reduce the chances of going deaf as they get older. A study of New England centenarians showed the one thing they had in common was a sunny disposition.

It seems likely that optimism and a happy disposition are likely to protect your brain against the ill-effects of ageing, too. You get to be brighter for longer if you're happy – that's enough to make anyone smile!

Success busts stress

The person who never made a mistake, never tried anything new.
Albert Einstein

We all have aims, ambitions and goals, whether they are to learn to play the piano or to dance the tango. We all know we have to take these things step by step – learning, then moving on. What is the ultimate goal at each stage? What is the fundamental aim that sums up all the stages in a learning process?

I have asked this question of countless students over 30 years, and remarkably they all come up with the same basic answer: 'To get better with every trial.' This sounds so obvious and so true that few people ever think to question it. Yet it is actually a recipe for failure, and a recipe for repeated stress that will take its toll on your brain over the years.

You may succeed the first time. You may succeed the second. Sooner or later, though, you will face a setback. Getting better with every trial just can't be done.

The key to success is to learn to work the way the brain works, and to learn the way the brain learns – and that is by continual feedback and adjustment. The point is that you never fail; you simply *receive feedback* which helps you move on.

This is a strategy for success. I call it TEFCAS:

1. **Trial**
2. **Event**
3. **Feedback**
4. **Check**
5. **Adjust**
6. **Success**

Trial: You have to begin by Trying something, whether it is throwing the ball in the air for your first attempts at juggling or trying out a new computer skill.
Event: When you Trial something, something – an Event – will happen. You may drop the ball or the computer may go blank.

Feedback: The Event will tell you something you didn't know before; it will give you Feedback – as you see your hand miss the ball, for instance.

Check: You compare the Feedback with what you did before. Your brain will Check how high you threw the ball, for instance.

Adjust: Using the Feedback and Check, you Adjust your strategy for the next attempt.

Success: This time you do much better. You might Succeed in catching the ball. Even so, this is still just another Trial, and with every Trial there is an Event and more Feedback, more Checking and more Adjustment. You found that the ball stung your hand when you caught it, for instance. Next time you will Adjust for that.

By thinking in terms of TEFCAS – looking at each setback as simply the feedback you need to check, adjust and move on – you can ditch stress and enjoy success!

SET THE RIGHT GOALS

I'm going to ask you to do something now that at first seems to have nothing to do with stress ... be patient and all will be revealed. Go and sit down for a few moments in peace and quiet and try to imagine your perfect day some years in the future in as much detail as possible, from start to finish. It can be as outrageous and fantastic as you want. Enjoy yourself. You might be on a tropical beach sipping cocktails or you might be drinking at the nineteenth hole after a perfect round of golf. It doesn't matter – let your fantasies run riot.

Life coaches often talk about the need to set goals in order to make progress in life. Write down what your goals in life are at the moment:

- **What do you want to achieve over the next seven days?**
- **What do you want to achieve over the next seven months?**
- **What do you want to achieve over the next seven years?**

Now think about that perfect day you imagined – how do the goals you have set yourself bring you closer to making that dream come true?

If you're like many people, you may now have a bit of a shock. Your goals don't seem to bring you any nearer to that perfect day at all!

In his book *The Motivated Mind* Raj Persaud cites a client of his whose chief goal in life was to be a novelist. The client was deeply frustrated because he could never quite finish a book. When Dr Persaud asked him about his perfect day, it involved tropical beaches, scoring the winning goal in the World Cup Final and being treated like a celebrity. There was nothing literary in it whatsoever. It was clear that he didn't really want to be a novelist at all. His fantasies revealed what he really wanted. No wonder, then, that he was feeling frustrated and stressed – he was setting himself the wrong goals in life and then feeling a failure because he didn't achieve them.

What's true of Dr Persaud's would-be novelist is true of many of us – we fail to identify our true goals in life and end up feeling stressed chasing the goals we think we ought to have. Once we know what we really want, however, we can move in the right direction. Then life becomes considerably less stressful.

Relax

Relaxing is a great way to combat stress. And as well as resting your body, it rests and restores your mind. When you relax, your brain has the opportunity to file away information you have been using. Think of it like mental housework: your brain needs to put away everything in a place it can easily access again. In general, it's when you are too busy to stop and think straight that you forget things, as everything piles up in your mental library and your brain can't track down the right information. It's times when you are frantically getting ready to go away on holiday with the family that you can forget something as vital as your passport!

In excess, stress itself can also interfere with your ability to recall information, as your mind tends to leap about between tasks or information and not focus on the task at hand. A well-rested mind is one that can concentrate and perform to perfection.

With this in mind, how can you relax – without even trying?

BREATHE

The quickest and most effective way to relax is to take control of your breathing. When you are stressed and anxious, your breathing becomes rapid and shallow. This keeps you on your toes and reinforces your anxiety. By deliberately slowing down and deepening your breathing, you can help yourself become more calm and relaxed.

If you find yourself becoming wound up at any time during the day, or before or after a pressure event, such as an interview or presentation, take a few moments to breathe deeply. Better still, try it several times a day, and you'll find yourself generally more calm and easy-going.

Some people find singing properly or doing voice exercises a very effective way of learning to control your breathing. By helping you to use your voice freely and richly, it also gives you extra confidence, which in turn helps take some of the stress out of life.

For a quick top-up, just practise breathing deeply 6 times in through your nose and out through your mouth, counting slowly up to 7 on each breath. Imagine yourself being as calm as possible as you do.

STRETCH AND RELAX

When you have time and space to practise properly, try this:

1. Stand up straight and relaxed with your legs placed firmly apart.

2. Roll your head gently around on your neck, first one way and then the other.

3. Relax your arms and gently whirl them around like windmills, one after the other.

4. Loll over gently at the waist, letting your arms and head hang down to the floor. Shake yourself gently loose. Now gradually straighten up, pulling yourself up vertebra by vertebra, starting with your coccyx and only bringing your head up slowly at the end.

5. Bend over again and wrap your arms around your body. Breathe in deeply through your nose, trying to take the breath as deeply into your body as you can, against the pressure of your ribs. Breathe out through your mouth and relax. Repeat for 7 breaths. Then come back up slowly again as before. If you find yourself feeling dizzy, sit down and relax for a while.

6. Lie down on the floor with your feet on a chair and your head comfortably on a pillow. Breathe in through your nose, trying to take the breath in to expand and spread your lower back across the floor. Breathe out slowly through your mouth, trying to reach the ceiling with your breath in your imagination as you do. Start by breathing out for a count of one, then two, then three, and so on, gradually building up until you can count as many as possible while still breathing out.

7. When you've finished, roll over gently on to your side, and then get up very slowly to a kneeling position. Finally, bring yourself upright again in the same way as before.

MEDITATION

Meditation has long been a part of religious and spiritual life, especially in Asia. Today, more and more people are adopting it in the West for its value in developing peace of mind and lowering stress. There is some evidence that regular meditation can have real health benefits, particularly in terms of age-proofing your brain.

Meditation involves switching off as much as possible from the constant buzz of stimuli that surrounds us. Scans of the brains of Buddhist monks well-trained in the art of meditation show they are able to effectively 'turn off' the areas of the brain normally associated with seeking stimuli. In some cases, meditation can dissociate the conscious brain from feedback from the sensors in the body that tell you where it is in space. The result can be a sensation of being disembodied or floating in space.

There are countless ways of meditating, and different approaches suit different people. Many people find it easiest to go to a class, where the teacher takes you through the steps. This is just one approach:

1. Wearing loose, comfortable clothing, sit relaxed and upright with your legs gently crossed in front of you. Sit against a wall if you find it hard to support yourself.
2. Shut your eyes and breathe slowly and deeply from your abdomen.
3. After a few minutes, spread your fingers and, with your arms bent, hold up your hands parallel in front of you, with the fingers pointing up.

4. Try to imagine drawing the 'energy of the universe' in through the tips of each finger in turn.

5. Now focus your mind on the spot between your nose and your upper lip and let go of any control over your mind. Simply relinquish control and let thoughts come in and out as they will.

6. After five to ten minutes, say 'Thank you' and allow a feeling of pleasurable gratitude to sweep across you.

7. Open your eyes gradually, and slowly get up in your own time.

VISUALIZATION

There is nothing like the imagination for getting a grip on your mind and either building stress and anxiety up or winding them down. Films, books and games can all stimulate the imagination and affect your stress levels. Different people relax by throwing themselves into different imaginary worlds.

In your imagination you are not simply a passive bystander, swept along on the journey any movie or novel takes you – you can use your imagination to devise your own journey and help yourself to relax, using a technique called visualization. It differs from daydreaming in that you control it.

Try this:

1. Find a place where you can be undisturbed.

2. Sit comfortably in an upright position and close your eyes.

3. Breathe deeply and slowly.

4. Imagine a scene in which you are completely happy and relaxed – for example, a tropical beach, a cosy fireside or a woodland glade.
5. Imagine it in as much detail as possible. Look around in your mind and study the colours, smell the scents and hear the sounds.
6. Be aware of the weather – the warmth of the sun or the fire on your face, the gentle breeze in your hair.
7. Whenever you need to relax, recall this scene in your mind.

When you become adept at this, you can also take the reverse approach and visualize in order to imagine yourself completely at ease in situations you might find stressful.

1. Sit down and relax as before.
2. Imagine the tricky situation that bothers you.
3. Imagine someone who looks like you coping with this situation in glorious style, carrying it all off to perfection.
4. Imagine this success in as much detail as you possibly can, playing the whole sense movie – the sights, the smells, the sounds, who is there, and so on.
5. Build up the picture of your doppelganger's success to the point where it seems absurd.
6. Now imagine yourself stepping inside your wonderful doppelganger's body.
7. Run through the whole scenario with you as the hero or heroine several times until it is firmly established in your mind.

SELF-HYPNOSIS

Self-hypnosis can also be a very good way of achieving a more relaxed state of mind. This exercise is built into The 7-Day Get Sharp plan – you will soon get the hang of it and enjoy its relaxing benefits.

Here's how:

1. Find a quiet place and quiet time of day where you are unlikely be disturbed and lie or sit down with your arms and legs unfolded.
2. Concentrate on breathing slowly and deeply in through your nose and out through your mouth.
3. Focus on a spot on the ceiling or wall opposite.
4. Begin to count backwards very slowly to yourself.
5. Move down through your body mentally from head to toe, telling each part silently to relax completely as you do.
6. Now imagine a special calm, comfortable place, such as a beautiful sunken garden or a heated pool in a tropical paradise at sunset.
7. Imagine walking down 10 steps into the garden or pool, counting each step carefully as you go.
8. When you've reached the bottom, look around you and try to imagine the beautiful, relaxing sensations you feel as you do.
9. Now try to imagine you're dealing with all life's problems in a calm, confident, relaxed fashion. Imagine in as much detail as you possibly can.
10. Repeat the previous step several times, each time

finishing by saying to yourself, 'I am increasingly calm and confident.'

11. Finally, when you are finished, count slowly down from 10 to 1, telling yourself it's OK to wake up now.

12. Wake up now, calmer and more confident.

SLEEP

Getting enough sleep is as important as taking time out to relax. A good night's sleep is essential for preserving the fitness of your brain and will give you the best chance to meet the coming day with a razor-sharp mind. The average person needs about six to eight hours of sleep a night – although it is also true that you need slightly less than this as you grow older – another advantage of age. Stress and sleep deprivation often feed into each other, since stress tends to make it harder for you to fall asleep at night and sleep deprivation in itself causes stress. Over time, too little sleep can dramatically interfere with the performance of your memory – something you obviously want to prevent! If you are not getting enough sleep, try going to bed 30 to 60 minutes earlier than your normal bedtime for a few days. This is normally enough to catch up on any sleep deprivation.

If, however, you suffer from insomnia you should seek the advice of your doctor. The chances are it is already impacting on your ability to remember and recall information – and if you are struggling to improve your memory scores this could be at the root of your problem. Prolonged periods of insufficient sleep can deplete the immune system, make you more accident prone and even cause depression – this can also reinforce a more negative outlook on life, which as we have already discussed, can contribute to your stress burden. The good news is that your memory and mood should automatically improve once you improve your sleep patterns. Tackle your sleep issues and everything else should fall into place.

Because stress management is so essential to maximize your brain power, The 7-Day Get Sharp Plan and The 7-Week Stay Sharp Plan both incorporate relaxation techniques. If you are not in the habit of setting aside time to relax, make it a priority to do so. Even a minute or two of deep breathing can start to work wonders. Often the best ideas and memories can come to you when you are in a state of relaxation as it is during these moments that your brain stores, processes and plays with the information is has received. Take some time out now and allow your mind to mull over the information in this chapter and how you can build in its stress-busting techniques. Then come back to the book, relaxed, refreshed and ready to embark on The 7-Week Stay Sharp Plan.

Chapter 8

The 7-Week Stay Sharp Plan

The 7-Day Get Sharp Plan that you followed in Chapter 4 was designed to kick-start your brain and get your mental juices flowing. The 7-Week Stay Sharp Plan builds on the progress you have already made and should bring you to a new level of mental agility.

Try to start it as soon as possible after completing The 7-Day Get Sharp Plan. For best results you need to set aside time one day a week for seven weeks. Ideally, set aside time the same day each week as this will help you get into a rhythm with the programme. The best time for you might be at the weekend. If you are unable to set aside the full amount of time needed in one session, you can break it down into more manageable time slots to complete throughout the week. Either way, make sure that you complete all the tasks within a week to get the full benefit of the programme. If circumstances interfere and make it impossible for you to stick to it week by week, just do your best to stick to the timings of the programme as closely as possible. You will still benefit from the plan even if you cannot work on it as intensively.

Every week you will be given a particular task to work on until the next part of the programme. As well as building on a particular skill practised that week, this task will help to get you into the habit of making mind-stretching games part of your daily life. As you work your way through each week, try also to consider which of the quick win techniques from Chapter 3 you could use to boost your performance. The Mind Map that you drew at the end of Chapter 3 to sum up all the techniques should help you.

Each of the seven sessions concentrates on a particular area of memory or mind-sharpening skill:

Week 1	**Quick-win Techniques – Refresher**	**2 hours**
Week 2	**Short-term memory**	**2 hours 50 mins**
Week 3	**Long-term memory**	**2 hours 55 mins**
Week 4	**Long-term memory**	**2 hours**
Week 5	**Memory and concentration**	**2 hours 15 mins**
Week 6	**Logical and spatial skills**	**2 hours 15 mins**
Week 7	**Creativity boost**	**3 hours 40 mins**

Finally and most importantly, make sure that you enjoy the programme – think of it as an adventure with your mind! The more fun you have with it, the more you will benefit from it – it's so much easier to apply yourself to something whole-heartedly when you find it entertaining.

How sharp have you become?

Before you start the programme let's take another look at how much progress you have made. Give yourself a score on a scale of 1 (easy) to 5 (real problem) for how easy you find it to remember these things:

Remembering names

☐ Someone you've just met
☐ Friends
☐ Family members
☐ Places such as restaurants you've visited
☐ Titles of books and movies you've seen

Remembering numbers

☐ PIN number
☐ Bank account number
☐ Familiar phone numbers
☐ New phone numbers
☐ Doing simple sums

Remembering dates

☐ Birthdays and anniversaries
☐ Appointments
☐ Household chores

Remembering where

☐ Where you put things (keys, remote controls, etc)
☐ Where you parked the car
☐ Directions

Remembering stories

☐ What you watched on TV last night, read in the
   papers, etc
☐ What you were just saying
☐ What the other person was just saying
☐ The right word for it

Add up your scores, and then see how you did:

20–30 Congratulations! You have no memory problems whatsoever. Keep looking for new challenges to keep your
brain in tip-top condition. Follow The 7-Week Stay Sharp
Plan to help keep your mind stretched and stimulated.

31–40 You're doing extremely well! Follow The 7-Week Stay
Sharp Plan to overcome the last of your mild memory
problems.

41–60 Pretty good! Although you still experience average memory problems, you can improve and aspire to more. Follow
The 7-Week Stay Sharp Plan to help you boost your performance and unleash the memory genius within!

61–80 You're making progress. You need to persevere with
the programme as you still have moderate difficulty
remembering things. Before you start The 7-Week
Stay Sharp Plan go back to Chapter 3 and revise the
quick-win techniques. If you haven't quite got the
hang of them it could be impacting on your perform-

ance. The second part of this assessment will also help identify any lifestyle issues that could be affecting your ability to remember things.

81–100 You are still experiencing severe memory problems. Return to Chapter 3 and make sure you have understood and learnt all of the quick-win memory techniques as knowledge and application of these alone should enable you to improve your score. The second part of this assessment will also help identify any lifestyle issues that could be affecting your ability to remember things. Make sure you start The 7-Week Stay Sharp Plan as soon as possible to overcome your severe memory problems.

Now compare your results with the test you did at the beginning of the book. Are you doing better overall? In which areas have you made the most progress? Are there still any areas that need work?

WHICH AREAS DO YOU STILL NEED TO WORK ON?

If you are doing better overall, congratulations! There is nothing more satisfying than knowing you are making progress. The beauty of your brain is that the more you use it the more mentally agile you become – and the sharper your brain is the more fun you can have with whatever you put your mind to, be it generating ideas, problem solving, fact-finding or number crunching. In fact, the more playful you are in your daily life, the easier it is to stay mentally agile and fit.

If you are still struggling to remember things in spite of The 7-Day Get Sharp Plan, identify the areas in which you have improved. If you have been suffering from memory problems for a while it will probably take more time to get yourself back on track. A very unfit person naturally needs more training before they can run a 200-metre sprint in a good time and in the same way an out-of-condition brain will take longer to get back on track. There may also be other external influences or lifestyle factors that are interfering with your performance. The questionnaire below should help you to identify these. Keep persevering with the programme in this book and you will soon start to make the progress you are looking for.

Circle a number for each answer, and then note your total score for each section.

Is your life under control?

1. Do you have a clear vision of what you want from life?
Yes (2)
Not sure/sometimes (1)
No (0)

2. Do you carry more than 50 pages of 'diary material'?
Yes (0)
Not sure/sometimes (1)
No (2)

3. Are you punctual?
Yes (2)

Not sure/sometimes (1)

No (0)

4. Do you use images, symbols and colours in your diary?
Yes (2)

Not sure/sometimes (1)

No (0)

5. Do you regularly feel stressed?
Yes (0)

Not sure/sometimes (1)

No (2)

6. Do you like planning?
Yes (2)

Not sure/sometimes (1)

No (0)

7. Do you plan regular breaks and holidays for yourself?
Yes (2)

Not sure/sometimes (1)

No (0)

8. Do you feel guilty if you're not working?
Yes (0)

Not sure/sometimes (1)

No (2)

9. Do you remember your life in individual years?
Yes (2)
Not sure/sometimes (1)
No (0)

10. Do you regularly review your life?
Yes (2)
Not sure/sometimes (1)
No (0)

11. Do you generally look forward to tomorrow?
Yes (2)
Not sure/sometimes (1)
No (0)

12. Do you feel threatened by your diary?
Yes (0)
Not sure/sometimes (1)
No (2)

Do you live healthily?

1. Do you eat (and like!) lots of sugar/salt?
Yes (0)
Not sure/sometimes (1)
No (2)

2. Do you regularly eat fresh vegetables and fruit?

Yes (2)

Not sure/sometimes (1)

No (0)

3. Do you eat a lot of refined foods?

Yes (0)

Not sure/sometimes (1)

No (2)

4. Are you considerably over- or under-weight?

Yes (0)

Not sure/sometimes (1)

No (2)

5. Do you take (and enjoy) regular exercise?

Yes (2)

Not sure/sometimes (1)

No (0)

6. Do you have regular health checks?

Yes (2)

Not sure/sometimes (1)

No (0)

7. Do you drink a lot?

Yes (0)

Not sure/sometimes (1)

No (2)

8. Do you regularly take recreational drugs?
Yes (0)
Not sure/sometimes (1)
No (2)

9. Do you grill rather than fry foods?
Yes (2)
Not sure/sometimes (1)
No (0)

10.Do you have a varied diet?
Yes (2)
Not sure/sometimes (1)
No (0)

11.Do you drink more than six cups of tea and/or coffee a day?
Yes (0)
Not sure/sometimes (1)
No (2)

12. Are you a smoker?
Yes (0)
Not sure/sometimes (1)
No (2)

Are you emotionally steady?

1. Are you self-confident?
Yes (2)
Not sure/sometimes (1)
No (0)

2. Are you able to cry?
Yes (2)
Not sure/sometimes (1)
No (0)

3. Do you often get annoyed?
Yes (0)
Not sure/sometimes (1)
No (2)

4. Do people generally consider you a happy person?
Yes (2)
Not sure/sometimes (1)
No (0)

5. Do you maintain friendships over a long time?
Yes (2)
Not sure/sometimes (1)
No (0)

6. Do you often feel helpless?
Yes (0)
Not sure/sometimes (1)
No (2)

7. Is life often a burden?
Yes (0)
Not sure/sometimes (1)
No (2)

8. Do you get along with your family?
Yes (0)
Not sure/sometimes (1)
No (2)

9. Do you say what you feel?
Yes (2)
Not sure/sometimes (1)
No (0)

10. Do you like to touch and be touched?
Yes (2)
Not sure/sometimes (1)
No (0)

11. Do you feel happy when others feel happy?
Yes (2)
Not sure/sometimes (1)
No (0)

12. Do you generally keep your fears to yourself?
Yes (0)
Not sure/sometimes (1)
No (2)

How sensually aware are you?

1. Do you enjoy dancing?
Yes (2)
Not sure/sometimes (1)
No (0)

2. Do you regularly enjoy films, plays, paintings and music?
Yes (2)
Not sure/sometimes (1)
No (0)

3. Can you recall visual information clearly?
Yes (2)
Not sure/sometimes (1)
No (0)

4. Can you recall smells and tastes clearly?
Yes (2)
Not sure/sometimes (1)
No (0)

5. **Do you recall sounds, tactile sensations and physical movements clearly?**
   Yes (2)
   Not sure/sometimes (1)
   No (0)

6. **Do you eat to live, not live to eat?**
   Yes (0)
   Not sure/sometimes (1)
   No (2)

7. **Are you sensual?**
   Yes (2)
   Not sure/sometimes (1)
   No (0)

8. **Do you enjoy playing with children?**
   Yes (2)
   Not sure/sometimes (1)
   No (0)

9. **Do you like your body?**
   Yes (2)
   Not sure/sometimes (1)
   No (0)

10. **Do you like nature?**
    Yes (2)
    Not sure/sometimes (1)
    No (0)

11.Do others consider you well-dressed?
   Yes (2)
   Not sure/sometimes (1)
   No (0)

12. Do you dislike driving?
   Yes (0)
   Not sure/sometimes (1)
   No (2)

How creative are you?

Get a pen and paper and a watch, then write down in just one minute, as fast as you can, all the possible uses you can think of for a rubber band.

TIP: Be as ridiculous and absurd as you like!

ASSESSING YOUR SCORE

Is your life under control?

18–24 Excellent. You enjoy a positive and balanced lifestyle and are working at something like maximum efficiency.

12–17 Good. There is still plenty of room for improvement. Are there any areas of your life that might be interfering with your overall mental agility?

6–11 Could and should try harder! The areas of imbalance in your life are probably affecting your overall mental performance. Try to identify the root causes of these areas of imbalance and take steps to address them.

0–5 You are not using anything like the full power of your brain and body. The areas of imbalance in your life are almost certainly affecting your overall mental performance. Try to identify the root causes of these areas of imbalance and take steps to address them.

Do you live healthily?

18–24 Excellent. You are giving your brain every opportunity to flourish.

12–17 Good. There is room for improvement, as you may not be looking after yourself quite as well as you think. Read Chapters 5, 6 and 7 to look for ways in which you can better support your mind and body.

6–11 You may be losing out mentally by underestimating the importance of physical health. Study Chapters 5, 6 and 7 again to identify ways in which you can better support your mind and body.

0–5 You are undermining your brain by abusing your body. Give your brain a chance! Study Chapters 5, 6 and 7 again to identify ways in which you can better support your mind and body.

Are you emotionally steady?

18–24 You are extremely emotionally mature.

12–17 Although you are pretty steady, you could settle down a little.

6–11 You wrongly undervalue yourself. Take another look at Chapter 7 and read over the sections about positive thinking.

0–5   You need to take steps to look after your overall emotional well-being. Start by returning to Chapter 7 and work your way through the positive thinking and relaxation techniques. You should also consider seeking professional advice to help you rebalance your emotional well-being.

How sensually aware are you?

18–24   Excellent. You live a well balanced, sensual, cultural and physical life and your brain benefits as a result.

12–17   You are sensually aware. There are blocks here and there.

6–11   You need a little more physicality in your life. Try some new physical activity such as a sport or dancing. Take time to enjoy food, music and other pleasures in life.

0–5   Your brain is being starved of sensory stimulation. Get out and do things that involve moving your body!

How creative are you?

This test was devised by E Paul Torrence. A typical score is 3–7. If you got 8–12, you're doing very well. If you got more than 12 you're a creative powerhouse.

Your results from each area of this questionnaire should help you to identify the emotional and lifestyle issues that could be limiting your overall mental performance. If you have been unable to improve your scores since you started the programme, it is quite possible that a lifestyle or personal issue is behind it. Address this and you should soon see your overall mental agility improve.

Stay Sharp – Week 1

Total time: 3 hours approximately

The first week of The 7-Week Stay Sharp Plan revises all of the quick-win techniques in Chapter 3 to make sure you have got the hang of them and can use them with ease. Make sure you take regular breaks to keep your mind fresh. Five minutes or so every 15 or 20 minutes is ideal.

MIND MAPS

Time: 10 minutes

Go back to page 57 to revise the key guidelines for drawing a Mind Map. The main things to look out for are that you add only one word to each branch and that your image sketches and words all sit on their own branches.

Now get your paper and coloured pens and draw a Mind Map of all the food and drink that you like.

Start with an image in the centre of the page that tickles your imagination, such as a sketch of a smiling face, a shopping basket or a person with a big round belly and get going.

Start with your main ideas, such as the different groups of foods, and let your ideas and your Mind Map expand from there.

CHUNKING

Time: 5 minutes

When you have drawn your Mind Map, take a look at all the information on it. In labelling your main branches you will have automatically grouped or chunked the information into various categories, such as 'sweet', 'savoury', 'vegetables', 'meat' and so on. Mind Maps are a fantastic natural chunking tool.

Let's take another look at how you can chunk information. Look at the list of words below, arrange them into meaningful groups and give yourself 5 minutes to remember them all. Cover up the words and see how many you can remember.

Shower gel	Dictionary
Apple	Chicken
Paper	Hair gel
Pencil sharpener	Fish
Muesli	Flapjack
Shampoo	Razor
Bananas	Rubber band
Computer	Flour
Nail polish	Post-it
Face flannel	

PATTERNS

Time: 5 minutes

Look for patterns in the following numbers to help you remember them. Give yourself 5 minutes to memorize them, then cover up the page and test yourself.

10661914
12367893
04436912
91101456
19195522

NUMBER TAGS

Time: 10 minutes

If necessary, return to page 66 to refresh your memory with the tags of the number shape and number rhyme systems.

Number shape

Time: 5 minutes

Use the number shape tags to memorize the following list of words. Remember to be as wildly extravagant with your image tags as possible. Then cover up the words and see how many of them you are able to remember.

1. Lid	6. Stars
2. Incense	7. Rubber band
3. Bottle	8. Grape
4. Pepper	9. Stapler
5. Phone	10. Dog

Number rhyme

Time: 5 minutes

This time use the number rhyme tags to memorize the following numbers. As before, imagine tagging the numbers together in as vivid and colourful a way as possible. It may also help saying the numbers out loud to find a rhythm and rhyme to the number groups. After 5 minutes, cover up the numbers and test yourself.

3863
54789
3427891
12090034
968621562

ALPHABET TAGS

Time: 10 minutes

The alphabet tag system (see page 69) is extremely useful if you have to memorize a long list of items or words. Give yourself 10 minutes to remember the list of words below.

A. Revolver
B. Wand
C. Orange
D. Spy
E. Salt
F. Swamp
G. Key
H. White
I. Mug
J. Tiger
K. Tissue
L. Seal
M. Knife

N. House
O. Park
P. Eagle
Q. Croissant
R. Candle
S. Dinner
T. Train
U. Business card
V. Hat
W. Doctor
X. Timer
Y. Venus
Z. Headphones

MNEMONICS

Acronyms

Time: 10 minutes

Make up acronyms to help you remember the following groups of words. Spend 5 minutes on each group, then test yourself to see how many you get right.

Group 1 – names of rivers in Germany

Rhine
Elbe
Danube

Main
Tauber
Neckar

Group 2 – names of Munros in Scotland

Ben Hope	Sgurr Mor
Saileag	Ben Lomond
Mount Keen	Devil's Point

Rhymes

Time: 5 minutes

Make up a rhyme about the first groups of words above, the rivers in Germany, to help you remember them.

Using first and last

Time: 2 minutes

Make a mental note of the names of the first and last Munros in the list above to help you to recall all of them successfully.

Method of loci

Time: 30 minutes

If you have not been practising this technique, you will first need to fix a series of locations in your mind that you can use as memory tags. An easy place to start is where you live. Alternatively you can use an imaginary location, perhaps an amazing palace or your idea of your dream home.

As you approach the house and enter it you can pick out objects that are memorable to you and will work as good tags. These might be as follows:

The gate leading to your house
A bush beside the front door
The door knocker
The rug in the hall
The staircase
The grandfather clock
A big velvet chair

Pick out memorable objects in your real or imaginary house on your visual tour. If you like, draw a Mind Map of all the objects or locations you have earmarked. The more locations you select as tags, the more things you will be able to remember.

Once you are familiar with your location tags, use them as often as possible. It may take a little time before they become second nature. The ease with which you can use this system afterwards will make it more than worth your while.

When you wish to use your location tags, make sure that you associate the item or object that needs memorizing as vividly as possible. Get all of your senses on board, since the more alive the image is, the easier it will be to cement it in your memory.

Start practising with this list of 20 objects you need to take on holiday. Allow yourself 5 minutes to remember them, then cover up the list and write down as many as you can.

Snorkel	GPS
Passport	Boxer shorts
Currency	Scissors
Swimming trunks	Shorts
Penknife	Flippers
Mosquito net	Sun cream
Diving mask	Camera
Shirts	Insect repellent
Sandals	First aid kit
Guide book	Energy bars

Now try memorizing this random list of words. Once again, give yourself 5 minutes before covering up the words and testing yourself.

Printer	Curry
Coffee	Suntan lotion
Highlighter pen	Cactus
Statue of Liberty	Snowflake
Horse	Ring
Fan	Crisps
Watering can	Knife
Charcoal	Boulder
Pheasant	Frog
Duvet	Fairy
Scarf	

GET MOVING

Time: 60 minutes

As you read in Chapter 5, physical exercise and body fitness is as important to brain fitness as mental exercises. Your next task of the day is to take an hour of gentle, physical exercise. Try going for a walk in the fresh air or, if that doesn't appeal, see page 160 for other exercise ideas.

MENTAL CUSHION: RELAXATION

Time: 30 minutes

Having given yourself a good mental workout, you now need to relax. Finish your brain-boosting day by finding a comfortable space where you won't be disturbed and spend 30 minutes practising the breathing technique for relaxation described on page 193 of Chapter 7.

Your task this week is to use the quick-win memory techniques as often as possible. Start by focusing on the techniques that appeal to you most – if you prefer the number rhyme tags to number shape tags feel free to practise this one more – then make a conscious effort to build the other techniques into your daily routine. It might feel like it's taking longer to remember things at first. Once you get into the habit of using the techniques it will take you far less time to memorize what you want to memorize – and of course it will be far easier to recall the information as well.

Stay Sharp – Week 2

Total time: 2 hours 50 minutes approximately
This week of The 7-Week Stay Sharp Plan focuses on your short-term, working memory and how you can continue to improve it.

MEMORY TONER

Time: 40 minutes (includes time for checking answers)

Number memory

Your first task is to really build up your ability to remember numbers in your memory. The average person can remember 7 or so. You should have been able to push up your score with The 7-Day Get Sharp Plan. Today, the aim is to build up your score far beyond what most people can achieve at any age.

Find yourself a quiet space and a comfortable chair. Make yourself a cup of tea or coffee and put on some music you can relax to.

What you will need:

- A pen and paper
- An address book (a traditional paper one or the one in your mobile) as a source of telephone numbers (if you run out of numbers, use a generic telephone directory)

1. Begin by opening up the directory and covering up all the numbers, leaving just the top number exposed.
2. Now remember it, cover it up and write it down. Use the same hand to cover the number as you do for writing, to avoid the temptation of simply writing what you see.
3. Reveal the second number. Remember it, cover it up, write it down.
4. Go down through the list for 10 numbers, then check your answers.

5. Now repeat the exercise trying to remember TWO phone numbers at a time. This is more challenging. Remember that telephone numbers always follow the same pattern, meaning the same rules apply when trying to memorize them – chunk the numbers and repeat them to yourself out loud to fix them clearly in your short-term memory. If you are finding it easy to memorize two telephone numbers at once, try three.

6. Spend 40 minutes on this task and aim to remember as many numbers as you can.

7. Take frequent breaks – a 3-minute break every 10 minutes or so should do the trick. Do something completely different such as changing the music or topping up your tea or coffee.

MEMORY TONER

Time: 5 minutes (includes time for checking answers)

Exercises that challenge your short-term, or working memory help prevent embarrassing episodes of forgetting something that you need to do or losing the thread mid conversation. Despite the popular belief that 'senior moments' like these are inevitable as you grow older, the truth is quite the reverse: if you keep challenging your brain you can – and indeed should – continue to improve your short-term memory. It's not about how old you are, it's about how fit your brain is.

Speed read the following passage about a typical day of things to remember. Give yourself no more than 45 seconds.

This morning I need to look out that DVD for my friend Anna as I'm seeing her this evening. While I make breakfast I want to listen to that item on the closure of the regional hospital on Radio Phoenix. It's supposed to be on at 8.20am and my friend Jenny is being interviewed. I need to take out the rubbish when I go out and look out the plastic bottles for recycling – not the paper, that's tomorrow. I must remember to ring the bank to check on that payment and I need to chase up my missing paint order as soon as I get to work. I'm meeting Paul for lunch. Oh yes, he asked if he could borrow that book on the birds of Argentina before his trip next month. I should take that with me, too. I need to leave at 1.50pm, though, to give me 10 minutes to pick up my coat from the dry cleaner's. Then after work I'm meeting Anna and Suzy at Barkers Bar on Calvin Street at 5.45pm to see Martin Scorsese's new film. I must ring up and see if there are tickets available. Now where did she say it was on …?

Now see if you can answer these questions:

1. What was the first thing I had to do this morning?
2. On what radio station was the programme I wanted to hear and what time was it on?
3. Was it the plastic or paper I needed to put out for recycling?
4. Who did I need to call when I got into work?
5. What did I need to remember for my lunch date with Paul?
6. Where is Paul going and when?
7. Who am I meeting after work?
8. Where am I meeting them?
9. What else must I do this afternoon?

Check your answers. How did you do? If you got more than 5, you're doing very well.

SENIOR MOMENT OR SIMPLY STRESSED?

Sometimes, even though you are normally very good at remembering things, it's possible to have days when you're more absent-minded or forget something really basic in your daily life. You'll probably find that this is most likely to happen when you are feeling tired, stressed or generally out of sorts. Here are a few things you can do to help:

1. In general, try to keep your space well organized with everything in its place. That way when something's out of place you'll see instantly.
2. Put items you need to remember in an unusual, prominent place on your way out to the street.
3. Keep an updated calendar and appointments diary – either in a paper diary or on a personal organizer, preferably both.
4. Keep a To Do list of tasks for each day and each week (a Mind Map tapped on the fridge is my personal favourite). Tick tasks off when they are completed.
5. Write reminder notes to yourself and display them in prominent places.
6. In the old days, people used to tie a piece of string round a finger or a knot in a handkerchief to remind them to do things. Perhaps strange nowadays, it is actually an effective technique. Things like this provide cues to jog the memory. Any similar cue can help you – putting on odd pairs of socks, stuffing a foreign coin in your pocket, moving a chair, and so on.

MEMORY TONER

Time: 5 minutes (includes time for checking answers)

A reliable witness

Every now and then people witness a crime or mishap and are asked to be witnesses. Most people are far less reliable as witnesses than they would like to think. How about you?

Try reading through this passage, taking no more than 20 seconds:

A young woman comes out of the newsagents wearing a pink coat. As she passes the grocers, she puts her wallet and a few coins in her pocket, stops and pulls her phone out. She is just putting the phone to her ear when a short young man wearing a hoodie, with the hood down, runs up to her, grabs her left arm with one hand and the phone with the other. As she opens her mouth to scream, the young man snatches away the phone and races off past the newsagent, leaving the girl in a state of shock.

Cover the passage. Now answer these questions put to you by the counsel for the defence. Answer each question fully before moving on to the next.

1. What was the girl wearing?
2. What did she have in her hand when she came out of the grocers?
3. Where did the alleged assailant come from?

4. What was he wearing?
5. Could you see his face?
6. Was he fat or thin?
7. What did he do first?
8. Which arm did he grab her with?

If you are really on the ball, you'll have noticed that question 2 was a trick. She came out of the newsagents, not the grocers. One of the reasons we can be slightly unreliable witnesses is that we often only see what we expect to see. This is why we can completely miss the unexpected as if it wasn't there.

Now try again. Can you do any better this time? As before, take no more than 20 seconds to read the passage:

A blue BMW was coming up Preston Street from north to south. There was a man driving. A woman and a man on the left of Preston Street – that's the east side – caught sight of the car and the man waved. The driver waved back. At that moment, two dogs came hurtling out of a doorway on the right side of Preston Street – the newsagents, I think it was. One was brown, the other was small and black. They both darted into the road in front of the car. The black dog got across the road safely. The car driver only just saw the brown one in time. As he swerved to avoid it, his car mounted the pavement on the left of Preston Street and smashed into a wall.

Cover the passage. Now answer these questions put to you by the counsel for the defence. Answer each question fully before moving on to the next.

1. What colour was the car?
2. Which way was it travelling along Preston Street?
3. Who waved first?
4. Which side of the street were the couple standing on?
5. Which dog got across safely?
6. Which side of the road did the car hit?
7. Was the driver of the car a man or a woman?
8. Where did the dogs come from?

REMEMBERING STORIES

Time: 30 minutes (includes time for checking answers)

Here's a much longer, more complicated passage to read. This time your task is slightly different. Take 10 minutes to read it carefully. When you come across what you think is an important fact or name, use your imagination and association to fix it in your short-term memory. For example, to remember the name of Tutankhamun's wife, Ankhesenamun, you could use a combination of chunking, image and pattern: the start of her name, 'Ankh', is the word for a tau cross, so you could image a young girl wearing a shiny ankh necklace; the middle part of her name is 'ese' and you could think of it as being 'easy' to remember; the final part, 'namun', is very similar to the end of Tutankhamun's. Play with the information in the passage to help you remember it as easily as possible.

While Aye, Maya and Horemheb were putting Egypt to rights, the young king Tutankhamun and his even younger wife Ankhesenamun were free to enjoy themselves. They went hunting birds in the delta marshes near Memphis, skimming through the reeds in light boats, or chasing ostriches in chariots across the desert near Thebes. Tutankhamun is said to have loved hunting with a bow and his bow and arrow were found in his tomb. It was not all fun, though. In a move calculated to appease those upset by the move to Amarna, Tutankhamun oversaw the building of a great Colonnade Hall in the temple at Luxor.

Things looked bright when Ankhesenamun became pregnant, and the future of the royal line seemed to be assured. Sadly, this baby miscarried, and then another. The parents were deeply distressed, and going against all tradition had both the foetuses mummified. Although there were mutterings about a family curse, the royal couple were still teenagers and there was plenty of time for an heir to appear. And then, quite out of the blue, Tutankhamun died, aged just 18 or 19 years old.

Ever since Tutankhamun's tomb was discovered in 1922, people have speculated about how and why the boy king died. Was he just a sickly young man – the victim of generations of inbreeding? Or was there something more sinister at work?

In a recent book, Egyptologist Bob Brier suggests that Tutankhamun was murdered. Brier argues convincingly that marks on an X-ray of the boy king's skull show that he suffered a severe blow to the back of the head – in a place where the blow could not possibly have been accidental. The Egyptian state information service, meanwhile, hint that the forensic investigation indicates that Tutankhamun was poisoned, and even name a murder suspect called Tutu, an official in Amenhotep III's court.

Bob Brier argues that if Tutankhamun was murdered, the chief suspects are his wily uncle Aye, who became pharaoh after his death, and the equally cunning General Horemheb, who became king when Aye died. Both Aye and Horemheb left texts declaring themselves innocent. On Horemheb's statue is a warning, 'Egyptian brothers, don't ever forget what foreigners did to our king Tutankhamun.' So it does seem the boy king was murdered.

Another twist to the tale comes from the discovery in Turkey of clay tablets from the Hittite court of King Suppiluliuma. On one of these tablets, known as the Seventh Tablet, the king's son tells of an extraordinary letter from the Queen of Egypt to his father. It is extraordinary both for its frantic tone, and because it is written to the Hittites, Egypt's traditional foes. In the letter, the Queen writes, 'My husband died. I have no son. But you, they say, have many sons. If you would give me one son of yours, he would become my husband. I will never pick out a servant of mine and make him my husband! … I am afraid!'

Could this Queen of Egypt have been Ankhesenamun, Tutankhamun's teenage widow? The timing suggests so. If it was, then she must have been very frightened and desperate to turn to Egypt's arch enemies for help. And who was the servant she was being pushed to marry? The turn of events suggest it was her ageing uncle Aye. A ring found in 1931 shows that Aye did marry Ankhesenamun – before she disappears entirely from history.

Ankhesenamun's frantic appeal to Suppiluliuma was so incredible that at first he did not believe it. He sent a chamberlain to Egypt to verify it, and the chamberlain brought back an Egyptian Lord Hani who would vouch for the Queen. In the meanwhile, she was getting desperate. Clearly the pressure for her to marry was on, and she wrote again,

'Why did you say "they deceive me," in that way? Had I a son would I have written about my own and my country's shame to a foreign land? You didn't believe me and said so! My husband is dead. I have no son! I will never marry a servant of mine. I have written to no other country but you. They say you have many sons; so give me one of yours! To me, he will be a husband, but in Egypt he will be king.'

Eventually Suppiluliuma was convinced and sent a son to marry the young Egyptian queen. As soon as the Hittite prince crossed into Egypt, he was murdered. The outraged Hittites immediately went to war. They were beaten by superior Egyptian forces and the plague. Who murdered the Hittite prince? Bob Brier suggests the most likely scenario is that Horemheb did the deed, acting in conjunction with Aye. For as the ring shows Aye married Ankhesenamun shortly after.

We will probably never know what happened to the young queen. If she was forced to marry Aye, it seems she died soon after. She has no tomb, and she is strangely absent from the tomb pictures of both Tutankhamun and Aye. Bob Brier thinks it is highly possible that Aye is implicated in the murder of Tutankhamun, the Hittite prince, and Ankhesenamun, too. If Aye was the culprit, he was already old and did not live long to enjoy the fruits of his crimes. He became king when he married Ankhesenamun. Within a few years, Aye too was dead. Horemheb followed him on to the throne, and ruled for 27 years, to be succeeded by his vizier Ramses. With Horemheb's death, the last of the key players in the strange Amarna episode was gone, and Ramses and his offspring moved Egypt back to the old ways, as if it all had never happened.

Now go and make yourself a coffee, come back, sit down and try and draw a Mind Map (see page 57) to summarize as much of the story as you can. Give yourself 15 minutes. Work hard to remember the overall pattern and as many details as you can. When you've finally exhausted all you have to say, reread the passage, then check it against the information on your Mind Map. Be as critical as you can. Where is it different? What were the biggest gaps?

GET MOVING

Time: 60 minutes
Last week you spent an hour of your day on the exercise of your choice. Now it's time to spend another hour – you can do the same routine or try something completely different.

MENTAL CUSHION: RELAXATION

Time: 30 minutes
Your final task of the day is to spend 30 minutes relaxing. As before, find a comfortable space where you won't be disturbed and practise the breathing technique for relaxation described on page 193 of Chapter 7.

TASK OF THE WEEK

Big story

Time: approx 3 hours (includes time for
viewing a 90-minute film, resting in between,
carrying out the task and checking answers)
Your Task of the Week continues to work your short-
term memory. If you've ever found your mind going
blank when someone asks you what a film or TV
programme you've just watched was about, this
should soon be a thing of the past.

The first part of the exercise is to watch a
feature-length drama of your choice that you have
never seen before – either on DVD or video tape or
at the cinema. Leave a gap of an hour – either for
you to get home or while you get on with other
tasks. Next draw a Mind Map of or write down the
story of the drama from beginning to end as fully
and in as much detail as you can. How much detail
were you able to recall? Were you able to
remember the names of all the main characters?
What about the more minor characters. Did you
remember the location? What about the twists of
the plot?

If you like, watch the film again to check you
remembered everything correctly.

Stay Sharp – Week 3

Time: 2 hours 55 minutes approximately
This week we are going to work your long-term, semantic memory.

MEMORY TONER

Time: 10 minutes (includes time for checking answers)

Recognition quiz
To make use of a semantic memory, your brain has to find where it is stored. This is much easier if there are clues or prompts to help it retrieve the memory. With a multiple choice quiz you are given the right answer among the wrong ones. All you have to do is recognize it. When multiple choice questions are set, the alternative answers may be very obviously wrong if the quiz is a simple one, or very close to the right answer, possibly tricking your brain into falsely 'recognizing' the wrong answer. In this first quiz, all the questions are of this kind.

Give yourself no more than 5 minutes to answer all the questions below. Put a tick beside the right answer.

1. **Who won the Oscar for best actress in 1978?**
    ☐ Diane Keaton, *Annie Hall*
    ☐ Meryl Streep, *Kramer v Kramer*
    ☐ Jane Fonda, *Coming Home*
    ☐ Louise Fletcher, *One Flew Over the Cuckoo's Nest*

2. **What is the world's biggest lake?**

- [ ] Lake Baikal
- [ ] Lake Victoria
- [ ] Lake Erie
- [ ] Lake Superior

3. **What was George Eliot's real name?**

- [ ] Mary Golding
- [ ] Anne Wildman
- [ ] Edith Evans
- [ ] Mary Anne Evans

4. **What relation was the Roman Emperor Nero to Claudius?**

- [ ] Son
- [ ] Nephew
- [ ] Stepson
- [ ] Cousin

5. **What is the capital of Kazakhstan?**

- [ ] Tashkent
- [ ] Dushanbe
- [ ] Samarkand
- [ ] Astana

6. **How is the mineral fulgurite made?**

- [ ] By precipitation of chemicals
- [ ] Volcanically
- [ ] By lightning strikes
- [ ] By marine deposition

7. Which is the largest muscle in the body?

- [ ] Deltoid
- [ ] Gluteus maximus
- [ ] Triceps
- [ ] Latimus dorsi

8. Which of these rivers is longest?

- [ ] Yenisey-Angara (Russia)
- [ ] Mackenzie (Canada)
- [ ] Mekong (Vietnam)
- [ ] Huang-Ho or Yellow (China)

9. Which country is the centre of Shia Islam?

- [ ] Pakistan
- [ ] Iran
- [ ] Iraq
- [ ] Saudi Arabia

10. Who is the voice of the buccaneer cat in the animated film *Shrek 2*

- [ ] Bruce Willis
- [ ] Antonio Banderas
- [ ] Orlando Bloom
- [ ] Kevin Spacey

11. What was the Greek name for the north wind?

- [ ] Skiros
- [ ] Zephyros
- [ ] Notos
- [ ] Boreas

12. **Which is the brightest star in the night sky?**
    - [ ] Sirius
    - [ ] Betelgeuse
    - [ ] Aldebaran
    - [ ] Arcturus

13. **What's the largest county in Ireland?**
    - [ ] Mayo
    - [ ] Galway
    - [ ] Kerry
    - [ ] Cork

14. **What is the most valuable monetary note?**
    - [ ] $1,000
    - [ ] €1,000
    - [ ] €5,000
    - [ ] $10,000

15. **Where is the world's largest art gallery?**
    - [ ] Paris
    - [ ] St Petersburg
    - [ ] Madrid
    - [ ] New York

16. **Who recorded the original version of the song 'Love Me for a Reason' covered by Boyzone?**
    - [ ] Bay City Rollers
    - [ ] Jackson 5
    - [ ] Osmonds
    - [ ] Fortunes

17. Which was Mark Twain's first successful novel?

☐ *The Adventures of Tom Sawyer*
☐ *A Connecticut Yankee in the Court of King Arthur*
☐ *The Prince and the Pauper*
☐ *The Adventures of Huckleberry Finn*

18. In which film did Gwyneth Paltrow star with Ewan McGregor?

☐ *Great Expectations*
☐ *Sliding Doors*
☐ *Emma*
☐ *Possession*

19. What is the world's second largest island after Greenland?

☐ Madagascar
☐ New Guinea
☐ Borneo
☐ Sumatra

20. What is syzygy?

☐ A medieval dance movement
☐ The mating behaviour of shore birds
☐ An alignment of planets
☐ An operation to remove an intestinal growth

21. Which of these is not a halogen?

☐ Astatine
☐ Bromine
☐ Guanine
☐ Iodine

22. When did Poland join the EU?

☐ 2001
☐ 2003
☐ 2004
☐ 2005

23. Terri Augelo and Craig Cook are the parents of which famous singer?

☐ Lauryn Hill
☐ Mary J Blige
☐ Beyonce Knowles
☐ Alicia Keys

24. Which is the highest mountain in the world after Everest?

☐ Lhotse
☐ Aconcagua
☐ Kangchenjunga
☐ K2

25. Where would you find a palimpsest?

- [ ] Under the skin
- [ ] In an ancient parchment
- [ ] In a medieval herbal
- [ ] On a knight's shield

26. Who said, 'Give me chastity and continence, but not yet'?

- [ ] Winston Churchill
- [ ] Casanova
- [ ] Woody Allen
- [ ] Saint Augustine

27. What are the world's biggest amphibians?

- [ ] Nile crocodiles
- [ ] Komodo dragons
- [ ] Chinese giant salamanders
- [ ] Cane toads

28. When the UK's Andy Green set the world land speed record in 1997, how fast was he travelling?

- [ ] 970.56 km/h
- [ ] 1,227.98 km/h
- [ ] 1,402.76 km/h
- [ ] 2,003.64 km/h

29. Japanese Shigechiyo was the oldest man ever on record. How old was he?

☐ 113 years 210 days
☐ 119 years 40 days
☐ 120 years 237 days
☐ 125 years 123 days

30. What is the most common element in the Universe?

☐ Iron
☐ Carbon
☐ Helium
☐ Hydrogen

31. Who became the first President of Iraq after the downfall of Saddam Hussein?

☐ Jalal Talabani
☐ Massoud Barzani
☐ Turgut Ozal
☐ Mahmoud Ahmadinejab

32. What part of the brain is a tough body?

☐ Cortex
☐ Cerebellum
☐ Corpus callosum
☐ Hippocampus

33. Grenadine and gin are mixed with what other alcoholic drink to make a Singapore Sling?

☐ Cointreau
☐ White rum
☐ Vodka
☐ Cherry brandy

34. What is or are ramsons?

☐ A small red fruit
☐ The bolts on a cannon
☐ Wild garlic
☐ An eighteenth-century term for cabin boys

35. What nationality was the composer Franz Liszt?

☐ Hungarian
☐ German
☐ Austrian
☐ Polish

36. Which of these was not a member of the Gang of Four?

☐ Yao Wenyuan
☐ Den Xaoping
☐ Jiang Qing
☐ Zhang Chunqiao

37. Who was the first Prime Minister of Australia?

☐ Alfred Deakins
☐ Edward Barton
☐ Sir George Reid
☐ Andrew Fisher

38. Who did Roger Federer beat to lift his first Wimbledon title?

- [ ] Andy Roddick
- [ ] Mark Philippoussis
- [ ] André Agassi
- [ ] Leyton Hewitt

39. In which Shakespeare play does Rosalind appear?

- [ ] *As You Like It*
- [ ] *Measure for Measure*
- [ ] *Twelfth Night*
- [ ] *A Midsummer Night's Dream*

40. What percentage of the vote do parties have to achieve to be represented in the German parliament?

- [ ] Unspecified
- [ ] 1 per cent
- [ ] 5 per cent
- [ ] 8 per cent

41. What is the busiest airport in the world?

- [ ] Heathrow, London
- [ ] Chicago O'Hare
- [ ] Hartsfield, Atlanta
- [ ] Chep Lap Kok, Hong Kong

42. Who wrote *Uncle Tom's Cabin*?

- [ ] Mark Twain
- [ ] Harriet Beecher Stowe
- [ ] Louisa May Alcott
- [ ] Harriet Martineau

43. How old is the Universe thought to be?

- [ ] 4.5 billion years
- [ ] 5.6 billion years
- [ ] 9.2 billion years
- [ ] 13.7 billion years

44. What is the currency of Ecuador?

- [ ] Sucre
- [ ] US dollar
- [ ] Peso
- [ ] Peseta

45. Who was the richest person ever?

- [ ] John D Rockefeller
- [ ] John Paul Getty
- [ ] Bill Gates
- [ ] Cornelius Vanderbilt

RECALL

Time: 10 minutes (includes time for checking answers)
When you have no clues to help you, finding the answer in your memory is much harder. Answer the following questions in no more than 5 minutes.

1. Who was captain of the first ship to sail around the world?
2. Who wrote the music for the film trilogy *The Lord of the Rings*?
3. What two lines follow in this song lyric, 'But through it all, when there was doubt, I ate it up and spat it out ...'
4. Where would you find the Koh-i-noor diamond?
5. Who was the terracotta army made for?
6. What was Lenin's real name?
7. In which city is the Taj Mahal?
8. What's the world's biggest fish?
9. What is the speed of light to the nearest km/second?
10. What are John Bardeen, Walter Brattain and William Shockley famous for?
11. What are the ingredients of pesto?
12. Who won the European Cup in 2005?
13. What is a radula?
14. What is the biggest planet in the solar system?
15. Who said, 'On the plus side, death is one of the few things you can do lying down'?
16. Who was elected President of Venezuela in 1998?
17. What is the highest mountain in Europe?
18. Who said, 'Hell is other people'?
19. In which country is the wettest place in the world?
20. Who flew the Command Module for the Apollo 11 Moon landing?
21. What Irish patriot was known as the Big Fellow?
22. How many pounds are there in a ton?
23. A group of which animals is known as a sleuth?
24. Where would you find Leonardo's Last Supper?
25. In which country would you eat pelmeni?
26. Who directed the film *Edward Scissorhands*?

27. Who was President of the EU in 2006?
28. Which chemical elements have just a single vowel in their name?
29. What are the four main bones in the human arm?
30. What are the largest states in A. India B. the USA?

LONG-TERM EPISODIC MEMORY

Time: 35 minutes

The memories that are most important to us, the memories that enrich our life and define who we are, are our episodic memories. Some of these are so powerful that they stay with us all our lives. Most, however, can fade with time. Usually they don't disappear altogether and you can normally recapture them if you put your mind to it. Sometimes the details are blurred, which makes it harder to know if you are remembering something as it was or imagining what it might have been like.

How well can you remember these things in your life? Give yourself 5 minutes to thinking about the questions below:

1. What colour was your first bedroom as a very young child?
2. How did you feel on your first day at school?
3. What was your most embarrassing moment as a child?
4. Who was your best friend at junior school?
5. What kind of car did your parents have when you were 9?
6. How did you spend your holidays when you were 10?
7. Who was your first romantic interest, ever?
8. Who was your first teacher at junior school?

9. What was the naughtiest thing you did as a child?
10. What was the bravest thing you did as a child?
11. What was your proudest moment?
12. What things did you pass on your route to junior school?
13. What was the first film or theatre show you ever went to see?
14. What was the most exciting day of your childhood?
15. What did your mum's kitchen smell like in the morning before you went to school?

These are very simple questions and the chances are you gave them each a very simple answer. You might have just said, for instance, that your first bedroom was blue. However, spend more time thinking about your room and a whole flood of other details would almost certainly come flooding back – objects in the room, your viewpoint, how you felt about it, and so on. In fact, it could even feel as if you were reliving the experience of being in the room. What is astonishing is just how fully you can remember things well and truly in the past if you give yourself time. The more often you try to recall the past and stretch your memory, the easier you will find it to remember episodes. You will also find that your memories will become more detailed.

The next 4 weeks of this 7-week programme all include a 15-minute session to explore, in detail, three of the questions above. Each time, find yourself a quiet place where you can shut your eyes and take yourself back in time completely. Don't worry if your mind wanders: it may well take you off down all kinds of interesting paths if you give it time. If you stray too far for too long, gently bring yourself back to the event in question and try to explore a different route.

Today you are just going to focus on the first three questions. Spend 10 minutes on each and try to recall the scenes in as much detail as possible, involving all of your senses. Try drawing a Mind Map as you go along to help you explore each episode.

1. What colour was your first bedroom as a very young child?
2. How did you feel on your first day at school?
3. What was your most embarrassing moment as a child?

KEEP YOUR MEMORIES FRESH

Try to make a habit of refreshing your memory for experiences, events and information you want to remember. You can do this in many ways, for example:

1. Start a Mind Map journal to help you remember the most significant episodes in your life.
2. Devote an hour or so every month to reliving one of your chosen episodes in as much detail as you can.
3. Brainstorm the details of the event on a blank page of your journal.
4. Gather any mementos you have.
5. Whenever there are family gatherings or friends' reunions, take a little time to share memories in detail.

5. Use triggers to help you: if there was a smell of onion on the day you are trying to remember, get an onion out and sniff it. If there was a particular piece of music playing, get hold of the music and play it. If it happened in a particular place, revisit the place if it's nearby.

By recapturing the memories in this way you should be able to remember them well whenever you want.

Keeping a Mind Map journal or even a simple diary will keep important memories fresh in your mind. A diary or Mind Map journal is a fail-safe back-up to your mental memory and a useful way of keeping your episodic memory toned.

If you don't wish to keep a Mind Map journal or diary, it's a good idea to take the time to recall the most memorable moments of the day just before you go to bed. Get the setting and context clear in your mind while they are still fresh. Mull over the event – who was there, what was said, how you felt and so on. That way it will be laid down clearly in your long-term memory as you sleep.

LONG-TERM PROCEDURAL MEMORY

Time: 30 minutes

Procedural memories are the memories you usually take for granted, the everyday skills that are so familiar you do them on autopilot, from making a cup of coffee to setting the DVD to record. Just how well do you know these tasks?

Your task is to make a cup of tea or coffee just as you do every morning. Try to do so entirely from memory without any of the objects to help you. If normally you make your cuppa in the kitchen, do this exercise in another room. Act out the process of making it in real time, trying to remember every single move you make and how you make it. Try to remember everything in as much detail and as accurately as you can.

- **Where are things in the kitchen? How do you move around them?**
- **How do you perform all of the little steps involved in making the coffee?**
- **How does it feel holding the various items you need? How do you move them?**

Re-enact the procedure as carefully and truthfully as you can. Don't try to exaggerate or mime. Simply remember it plainly as it really is. Take your time to remember every little detail. When you're satisfied that you've got the process spot-on, go into the kitchen and actually make that tea or coffee. As you do, check out your movements. How close were you to the real thing in the exercise? What mistakes did you make? Try this exercise with a few other familiar tasks. For example:

1. Taking a bath or shower
2. Ironing an item of clothing

3. Tying a tie or bow tie
4. Cooking an omelette
5. Cleaning your shoes

You'll find yourself becoming much more aware of the way you do things, and this awareness can exercise your memory.

GET MOVING

Time: 60 minutes

The next part of your brain workout is to train your entire body. Spend an hour doing the exercise of your choice, whether it's a walk in the fresh air, a bit of Tai Chi in the garden or a number of lengths at your local swimming pool.

MENTAL CUSHION: RELAXATION

Time: 30 minutes

As before, the final part of your brain-boosting day is to relax for 30 minutes. Return to your comfortable space where you won't be disturbed and practise the breathing technique for relaxation as described on page 193 of Chapter 7.

TASK OF THE WEEK

Memory toner

Time: 10 minutes plus time to get to venue of choice

This week your task is to take yourself off to a café, a museum or park you don't visit very often. Give yourself 10 minutes to memorize the short poem below. If you prefer, choose a different poem or short story to learn.

Had I the heavens' embroidered cloths
Enwrought with gold and silver light,
The blue and the dim and the dark cloths
Of night and light and the half-light,
I would spread the cloths under your feet.
But I, being poor, have only my dreams
I have spread my dreams under your feet;
Tread softly because you tread on my dreams.
William Butler Yeats

Make a note in your diary to sit down at home to try and recall the poem in three days' time. When it comes to reciting it, visualize where you learned it in as much detail as possible. You should find the visualization of this episodic memory helps you remember.

Stay Sharp – Week 4

Time: 3 hours approximately

This week we are going to focus on your long-term sensory memory. All the input to your brain comes through your senses, and the quality of your thinking is partly limited by the quality of the input. This is why it is vital to keep your senses as finely tuned as possible.

We talk about the five main senses, sight, hearing, taste, smell and touch, as if they are fully independent of one another and easy to distinguish. Our brains, however, are programmed to give us an overall awareness of our surroundings. To register something fully with one sense, we often have to make a conscious decision to focus on that sense. Training your senses to focus can dramatically enhance your perception. To an untrained ear, for instance, there are rarely more than four different birds audible in a forest. To the practised ear of a birdwatcher, however, there may be ten or more. Training your senses to concentrate in particular ways can dramatically enhance the intensity with which you perceive things.

FOCUS YOUR SENSES

Time: 10 minutes

Find a comfortable place to sit down at home, and spend 1 minute focusing on each sense.

Hearing

Time: 1 minute

Shut your eyes and listen carefully to all the sounds you can hear.

> Can you identify all the sounds?
> Where are the sounds coming from?
> Are there any sounds that are just on the limits of your hearing?

Sight

Time: 1 minute

Open your eyes and look at everything as if for the first time.

> Scan around the room taking everything in.
> Focus on particular things in turn.
> Is there anything you haven't noticed before?

Touch

Time: 1 minute

Shut your eyes again and focus on the sensations coming from all over your body.

> Can you feel the air moving?
> Can you feel the pressure of your body on the seat?
> Can you feel your clothes?

Now try moving your hands slowly and feeling different things – your clothes, your face, the chair and so on.

> What different textures can you feel?
> Do things feel hotter or colder?
> Do things feel soft or hard, smooth or rough?
> Can you identify different surfaces easily?

Smell

Time: 1 minute

Keep your eyes shut and sniff the air gently.

> Can you smell moisture in the air?
> Can you smell traffic fumes?
> Are there any cooking smells?
> Can you smell natural things such as trees and flowers?
> Is there a smell of rubbish, or industrial activities?

Even if there are no obvious smells, you'll be surprised by how much you can smell if you concentrate for long enough. It often takes time to identify a particular smell. If you can't, open your eyes, get up and see if you can trace its source.

Taste

Time: 1 minute

Now shut your eyes again and concentrate on taste. Roll your tongue around your mouth.

Are there any identifiable tastes?

Can you taste your own saliva?

Are there any lingering flavours of your last meal?

Now lick your finger and concentrate on its taste. You'll be amazed at how intense the flavour is.

THE FULL EXPERIENCE

Time: 5 minutes

Take an apple. Look at it very carefully. Examine any colour variations, its gloss, any blemishes.

Pick it up and turn it over in your hand. What does it feel like – smooth, waxy, dry, rough? Now sniff it. What does it smell of? Can you smell the tree it came from?

Bite into it with relish. What's the texture like – crispy or flowery? What does it taste like – sweet or sharp?

TIP: Try and practise these exercises regularly whenever you get the chance. You could take a moment to shut your eyes and take in the sounds and the smells, when travelling on the train or bus. Or you could pause briefly to look around at the things in your office or home as if for the first time.

EPISODIC MEMORY REFRESHER

Time: 15 minutes

Last week you had to try and recall three scenes from your past. This week try to recall all the details surrounding each of the questions below.

Find a quiet place where you can shut your eyes and take yourself back in time completely. Try to recall each scene in as much detail as possible, involving all of your senses. You may find it helpful to draw a Mind Map as you go along to help you explore each scene as fully as possible. Don't worry if your mind wanders: it will naturally take you down all kinds of interesting paths if you give it time. If you stray too far for too long, gently bring yourself back to the event in question and try to explore a different route. Spend 5 minutes on each question.

1. Who was your best friend at junior school?
2. What kind of car did your parents have when you were 9?
3. How did you spend your holidays when you were 10?

SENSORY MEMORY STRETCHER

Time: 85 minutes

Vision

Time: 15 minutes

Because our visual memories are so strong, we often overestimate just how accurate they are. We imagine what we see in our memories to be how it really is. This is not always the case, even with things we see all the time.

Try to visualize something you see everyday, such as your home from the outside, or your desk at the office. Now try to draw it as accurately as possible. Don't worry too much about your drawing skills. Be diagrammatic. The aim is to make a plan of where you remember everything to be rather than test your artistry.

Check how accurate you were against the real thing later. You'll be surprised how much you accurately remember. How many things did you get in the wrong place or miss out altogether? Did you add anything that wasn't there at all?

Sound

Time: 30 minutes

As we all know, there is a difference between hearing something and listening – and what separates the two is usually linked with concentration. If you work or live in a noisy environment, you hear (and ignore) a whole range of sounds in order to focus on the task at hand. Similarly, although you might be less inclined to listen to someone asking you to put out the rubbish, you would nearly always pick up on someone offering you a drink!

This aim of the next exercise is to get you to bring more awareness to everything you hear and to listen to it.

Hear anything new?
Time: 10 minutes

Sit in a chair and simply listen to all the sounds around you – even an empty house makes its own noises. What sounds have you heard that you don't normally register?

Tune into the radio
Time: 20 minutes

Get some coloured pens and paper and tune into a serious, low key talk programme or drama on the radio. Keep the volume quiet – only just loud enough for you to hear clearly and focus hard on what is being discussed.

As you are listening, draw a Mind Map to help you pick up on all the key information. Your Mind Map will help you listen more carefully and pull out the salient information.

Touch

Time: 30 minutes

Because we live in such a visually stimulating world, we don't always appreciate how our sense of touch can inform us about the world. Babies are far better at this than us and are forever exploring how something feels, most commonly by putting whatever it is into their mouths.

The exercises below will help you rediscover the level of information you can glean through touch alone.

Feel the money!
Time: 15 minutes

Put a variety of coins – at least five different values – in your pocket or a bag. Now put your hand in and try to identify them by touch alone. Pull the coin out to verify your identification, then put it back.

If you found this easy, try the same exercise including any foreign coins you picked up from trips abroad.

Think about what criteria you might use to distinguish them – size, thickness, milled edges and so on.

Now see if you can identify the sides of each coin – heads or tails?

Once you get the knack of this coin exercise, it's time to try something a little trickier. This is about touch and the accuracy of your spatial perception.

Potato fingers

Time: 15 minutes

Get a large bag of small potatoes – new potatoes are ideal. Take out six potatoes of different sizes and arrange them in a row in random order.

Now with your eyes firmly on the first potato in the row, try to pick out a potato of identical size from the bag by feel alone.

When your hand finds a potato of the right size, without looking at it, pull it out and put it on the table behind you.

Repeat for all the other potatoes in the row.

When you have what you think is a match for all six potatoes, compare the potatoes you pulled out with the potatoes in the original row and see how you did.

TIP: If you find yourself getting too good at this, try with fruit or vegetables of much more similar sizes, like cherries.

Taste and scent

Time: 10 minutes

Like your memory, you need to keep training your senses of taste and smell to keep them sharp. This is particularly true if you smoke since smoking damages the sensitivity of both. Connoisseurs of good food and drink – wine tasters, for instance – are well known for their ability to make very subtle distinctions in flavour well into old age. This is because they continue to train their palates.

The tongue can only make broad distinctions between five different tastes – sweet, sour, salty, bitter and savoury, which is why most of the subtle distinctions on flavours are down to their aroma – your nose can distinguish approximately 10,000 aromas. For this reason it is your nose that holds the most scope for training. The aroma of a raspberry, for instance, comes from the interaction of over 300 different chemicals. Although scientists can make a rough approximation of a raspberry scent with just a handful of chemicals, it is so rough that even a relatively untrained nose can tell it's not real. Experts can distinguish between different kinds of raspberries by smell alone.

Start paying attention to the smell of your food. Relish its aroma before you chew and swallow and try to identify the different aromas in it. You could even make yourself a connoisseur of a favourite food or drink. What more pleasurable way could there be of keeping your senses of taste and scent honed? It doesn't need to be wine. It could be whisky, cheese, coffee, different varieties of bread, or particular fruits – anything that takes your fancy.

You may ask why it is so important for your memory to keep your senses of taste and smell well trained. The answer is because both these senses are extremely powerful for establishing and recalling memories. How many times have you walked down the street, smelt a passer-by's perfume and thought of someone you know? If you like that person, the chances are the smell will make you feel happy. Equally, if you do not you will probably have a negative reaction to that smell. This is why returning somewhere with a very distinctive smell, for example your school, can trigger memories and emotions that may have lain dormant for years.

Savour and smell

Every time you eat or drink something for the rest of the day, spend a minute of two inhaling its aroma and trying to pick out all the different aromas that make up its identity. Even if you are simply drinking a glass of water, carefully sniff the glass and consider the texture and flavour of the water. There is a huge difference, for example, between tap and bottled mineral water in terms of texture and taste. When you eat your next meal, work hard to identify the different spices and herbs that have been used to season it. Take time to chew each mouthful and really appreciate what you are eating. This makes for a more sensually satisfying experience and it is also better for your overall digestive process.

GET MOVING

Time: 60 minutes

Now it's time to get your body moving with an hour of exercise. If you have chosen very gentle exercise forms for the first three weeks, consider pushing yourself a little further today. For example, if you have been going for a walk, try to walk a little further and a little faster. Make sure you choose a different route – your brain loves variety!

MENTAL CUSHION: RELAXATION

Time: 30 minutes

For the last three weeks you've been practising the relaxation exercise on page 193. This week, try the stretch and relax routine on page 188.

Time: 20 minutes a day
Your task this week is to continue to bring awareness to your senses. For the next four days try to do the following:

Sight. Spend 5 minutes visualizing a scene in your everyday environment then check how accurate you are against the real thing. You should find that you get more and more accurate each time you perform this exercise.

Sound. Spend 5 minutes sitting with your eyes closed listening to all the sounds going on around you. Do this in different places each time, for example in bed, on public transport or sitting in a park.

Touch. Spend 5 minutes repeating the exercise on page 261, each time using a different fruit or vegetable, for example carrots, cherries or walnuts.

Taste and smell. Every meal, take time to linger over the taste and aroma of what you are eating and work hard to distinguish the different seasonings that make it taste as it does.

Stay Sharp – Week 5

Time: 2 hours 15 minutes approximately

This week looks at how you can improve your powers of concentration – a key part in improving the overall performance of your memory. We will do this in three ways:

1. Focus

Focusing improves the strength of the input to your brain and boosts the number of neural connections it makes.

2. Amplify

Amplifying brings more neural networks into play by adding meaning, emotion, context, and so on.

3. Tag

Tagging involves making links to make recall easier.

IMPROVE YOUR FOCUS

If you were able to carry out all the sensory memory exercises last week, your focus should have already significantly improved. Let's look at how you can improve it further still.

How focused are you?

Some people are so focused that they verge on the obsessive. Others have their head in the clouds so much that someone could drop dead beside them and they wouldn't notice. Where on the scale do you fall? Try answering this test to identify whether you have a problem.

Score:
  2 points for never
  1 point for sometimes
  0 points for often.

1. I don't notice the weather.
2. I'm caught by surprise.
3. I daydream during conversations.
4. I watch TV while eating.
5. I find it hard to give strangers directions around my neighbourhood.
6. I get distracted by household chores that could wait.
7. I try to do several tasks at once.
8. I forget minor appointments.
9. I have music or the radio on all the time.
10. I get bogged down by unimportant tasks.
11. People think I'm scatterbrained.
12. I fail to hear things, even though my hearing is good.
13. I'm tired during the day.
14. I can't stick at a task for long.
15. I don't sleep well.
16. I eat quickly.
17. I miss my stop on the bus/train.
18. I'm anxious for no reason.
19. I don't find many things interesting.
20. I forget items on my shopping list.
21. I notice when friends have a haircut.

28–42 You are very good at focusing – maybe just a little too good! You could afford to relax and let your mind wander every now and then.

14–27 You can concentrate when you put your mind to it. Often you don't, being distracted by trivial things, or having moments of absent-mindedness such as entering a room then wondering why you are there. The exercises below should make all the difference.

0–13 You are away with the fairies! Maybe you are just a dreamer, or maybe you are going through a time of great stress. Sometimes we stop paying attention to the world around us when life's problems seem too much. This is especially so if you're suffering from lack of sleep. Before the exercises here will make much difference, you need to deal with the stress. Do one of the stress-busting techniques in Chapter 7 then take yourself out for a small treat. Slow down and give yourself plenty of time to enjoy your meals and sleep. Only then should you try the exercises below.

How observant are you?

Time: 3 minutes

How much do you notice about the world around you? Without looking, see if you can answer these questions about your everyday world:

1. What items do you have on the shelf in the bathroom?
2. What brand of soap do you have?
3. Does your lounge door handle turn clockwise or anticlockwise to open?

4. What colour is your toothpaste tube?
5. What make of TV do you have?
6. Where are your keys at this moment?
7. If you work in a city, how many newsagents are there in the street where you work?
8. What's the name of your nearest shop?
9. What colour are the walls/brickwork of your neighbour's house?
10. What kind is the nearest tree to your house?

Now check your answers as far as you can. If you got more than 7 right, you're clearly very observant and focused. Well done. If you got less than 3, you're letting the world go by without hardly noticing. The next section will help you work on your observation skills and learn to focus more.

What's motivating you?

Interest and focus go hand in hand – if you are interested in something you are far more likely to give it your full attention. If you can identify what is motivating you to concentrate on the task at hand, it will be far easier to remember it. For example, if you decide to learn a new foreign language you can motivate yourself with the promise of a holiday in a country where it is spoken. Setting yourself goals and rewarding yourself when you achieve them is a great way to find personal motivation and focus.

Being focused and engaged in what is going on around you is also a habit that you can cultivate. The following exercises should help you.

Multi-tasking

Time: 3 minutes

Try reading this passage at the same time as counting silently in your head:

Once, the ancient lands of Gondwana and Laurentia had been brown and barren. At last, they were filling with life. The lycopods were now growing as tall and straight as trees. Vast forests of their green and scaly stems were spreading through the swamps.

Here and there in the damp ground between them stood ferns of incredible size, like living telegraph poles. Their smooth ribbed stalks were like fat bamboo. Their feathery fronds were delicate as green butterflies as they waved up and down in the moist air.

In the shifting shadows beneath, a thick undergrowth of smaller lycopods and ferns flourished along with strange little leafless plants called horneophyton – perhaps because they looked rather like a deer's horns.

All kinds of tiny animals lived here already. Spiders and scorpions, snails and slugs, centipedes and millipedes ... and insects, millions of insects. These animals were everywhere. Crawling over leaves. Scurrying up stems. Darting through the air. Dropping into the water. Their ceaseless activity filled the primeval wood with a constant buzz.

At this time, 370 million years ago, there was nothing to disturb the peaceful lifestyle of these tiny creatures. For most of them were plant eaters, quite happy to browse on the lush tropical vegetation. There were no giant hunters to send them dashing for cover – no birds, no reptiles, no shrews or mice, or anything else to threaten them with sudden death.

All that changed when the tetrapods arrived ...

Now answer the following questions:

1. What were the names of the two ancient lands?
2. How did horneophytons get their name?
3. How long ago did this scenario change?
4. What happened to make it change?

Because you were also trying to focus on counting, it is quite possible that you didn't manage to accurately answer many of the questions. This is because very few of us can really multi-task effectively.

The more you multi-task, the more chance you have of interrupting the memorization process. In general, you can hold things in your working memory for 30–80 seconds – just long enough to carry out the task at hand. If your thoughts are interrupted during that time, the memory is interrupted and easily lost. This why you can go from one room into another to look for something only to find that you've forgotten what you came in for by the time you get there. This not because your memory is failing you, it's simply because your thoughts have been interrupted en route. This is why the brief interruption of a phone call or a shout from the street can make you lose your train of thought.

Interruptions and multi-tasking are disruptive to your memory which is why you should aim to perform tasks sequentially, rather than at the same time. Try to discipline yourself to complete each task before you move on. Try also to avoid being forced to multi-task just to please others. If someone interrupts you, practise politely asking them to wait until you're finished.

In the meanwhile, these next exercises will help you practise concentrating in the face of interruptions and distractions.

Focusing: working memory

Time: 5 minutes

This focusing exercise uses your working memory. Here is a list of all the months, with their associated gemstones and flowers, except the list is in the wrong chronological order.

Turn on the television and tune into a lively programme (keep the volume at your normal level). Sitting close to it, give yourself 5 minutes to arrange the information below in chronological order and to memorize the information for each of the months.

April	Diamond	Daisy, sweet pea
October	Opal, tourmaline	Calendula, cosmos
December	Turquoise, zircon	Holly, narcissus, poinsettia
August	Peridot, sardonyx	Gladiolus, poppy
May	Emerald	Hawthorn, Lily of the Valley
January	Garnet	Carnation

June	Alexandrite, moonstone	Honeysuckle, rose
February	Amethyst	Primrose, violet
November	Topaz	Chrysanthemum
March	Aquamarine, bloodstone	Jonquil, violet
September	Sapphire	Aster, morning glory
July	Ruby	Larkspur, water lily

TIP: Try drawing a Mind Map or using the alphabet tag system.

Focusing: semantic memory

Time: 5 minutes

The next exercise uses your semantic memory. Remember as many words as you can in each of the following categories. As before, sit next to the television with it switched on and playing quite loudly.

Reptiles	Countries of Africa
Cities in Italy and Spain	American rivers
Composers	Tropical birds
Makes of cars	Animated films
Kinds of wine	Vegetables

TIP: Drawing a Mind Map will make this task easier.

TIPS TO HELP YOU FOCUS AND STAY ENGAGED

Try to adopt the following habits to help you in your daily life:

1. Make a point of learning something new every day. Read a newspaper article properly, take the trouble to look up some background information on your houseplants – whatever you choose. Make it a priority to give your mind some new information to play with.
2. Share what you have learned with other people.
3. Try new things as often as you can. Cook at least one new recipe a week. Vary your route to work. Listen to some unfamiliar music. Read an author you've never read before.
4. Make plans of tasks you can achieve, then carry them out.
5. If you catch your mind wandering, bring it back to full attention by looking for something that interests you about the situation at hand. For example, if you are talking to someone and finding that you are focusing more on how large their nose is rather than on what they are saying, look instead for a point in what they are saying to which you can respond – or use to steer the conversation towards what does interest you.
6. Respect your mind if you really are too tired or too stressed to pay attention. Make a clean break of the task at hand and take a rest. Try one of the

relaxation techniques in Chapter 7 to help you restore your sense of equilibrium.

7. Keep your powers of observation honed by being on the lookout for anything new in your neighbourhood, whether it is a new restaurant, a freshly painted house or a new road sign.

EPISODIC MEMORY REFRESHER

Time: 15 minutes

Last week you had to try to recall three scenes from your past. This week try to recall all the details surrounding each of the questions below.

Find a quiet place where you can shut your eyes and take yourself back in time completely. Try to recall each scene in as much detail as possible, involving all of your senses. You may find it helpful to draw a Mind Map as you go along to help you explore each scene as fully as possible. Don't worry if your mind wanders: it will naturally take you down all kinds of interesting paths if you give it time. If you stray too far for too long, gently bring yourself back to the event in question and try to explore a different route. Spend 5 minutes on each question.

1. Who was your first romantic interest, ever?
2. Who was your first teacher at junior school?
3. What was the naughtiest thing you did as a child?

AMPLIFY AND TAG

The bigger and brasher things are when they happen – the stronger the emotion you feel, the bolder the colours, the louder the noise, the more outrageous the circumstances – the better they stick in your mind. This is because when you amplify events and information they capture your imagination and, as we have already observed, if you can get your imagination on board it is a whole lot easier to remember anything you want.

Seeing big

Time: 10 minutes

Visual amplification is particularly important, since most people heavily rely on the sense of sight.

Let's say you would like to remember a particularly important date or appointment. To help fix it in your mind, scrawl it in your diary in the biggest, boldest and most colourful letters you can – surround the entry by stars or weird shapes, whatever you choose. Make sure you also write in the time and the date as although the diary gives you the date, your memory will latch on to it more easily if you write it down yourself. Even better than a diary entry, display a giant post-it note with the date and event in giant letters somewhere prominent around the house. Keep moving the note to a new place every day – it is amazing how quickly your eye becomes habituated and fails to notice the most obvious things if they don't change.

To see how effective amplification can be, copy this list of words quickly and neatly on to a sheet of paper:

Concrete	Sash
Normal	Slide
Underground	Abstract
Vertical	Brother
Tree	Sedge
Shop	Internal
Barbaric	Rhapsodic
President	Road
Gargantuan	Clinical
Even	Coffee

Now cover up your list and, using the tag system of your choice from Chapter 3 (alphabet tags, number tags or the method of loci), give yourself 5 minutes to remember as many of the words as you can. When you tag the words to your system of choice, make sure you do so in as imaginative and outrageous a way as possible.

Without the tag systems, most people will struggle to remember more than 10 of the words. With the help of amplification and the memory technique you should be able to remember ALL 20 of the words quite easily.

Try the same exercise again with the list of words below, only this time get a big sheet of paper and a set of coloured pencils. As you memorize each word in turn, scrawl them on the paper in huge letters and sketch a very rough icon into or next to the word that will help you link it to your tag system. Work quickly, choosing a different coloured pen and a different style of lettering for each word. As before, give yourself no more than 5 minutes to remember them all.

Aftermath	Bargain
Day	Elephantine
Heart	Green
Arm	Meaning
Body	Special
Cooking	Relevant
Street	Usual
Business	Meeting
Weather	Western
Sky	Brief

Cover up the list and your sketches, then see how many words you can remember. The chances are you found it even easier to remember them because you actually created a brightly coloured image of each of the words.

You can apply the same technique to any things you want to be sure to remember, such as:

1. the key facts for an essay
2. the essential elements of your business plan
3. the things you need to buy at the shop
4. things you need to remember for your holiday
5. ideas for gifts
6. a speech or presentation

Sounding big

Time: 4 minutes

When it's not possible or relevant to exaggerate visually, you can try amplifying the sound of what it is you wish to remember instead. Try remembering these four lines of poetry by reading them over three times silently. Give yourself no more that 2 minutes.

> Behold her, single in the field,
> Yon solitary Highland Lass!
> Reaping and singing by herself;
> Stop here, or gently pass.

Now cover the book and see how well you remember them. How well did you do? Was it harder to remember than you thought? Now try the second four lines of this famous poem by William Wordsworth called 'The Solitary Reaper'. This time, however, try singing the lines out loud very loudly, again going through it three times. Give yourself no more than 2 minutes.

> Alone she cuts and binds the grain
> And sings a melancholy strain.
> O listen! for the Vale profound
> Is overflowing with the sound.

Now cover the book and see how well you remember the lines. The chances are you found it much easier this time – in fact you should have remembered the lines perfectly.

You can apply the same technique to other things you need to remember quickly:

1. **Telephone numbers**
2. **People's names**
3. **Key points or sentences in a speech**
4. **Key points in a presentation**
5. **Poetry**
6. **Shopping lists**
7. **To do lists**
8. **Essay topics**
9. **Handy quotations**

All singing, all dancing

Time: 3 minutes

The more senses you can bring into amplification, the more memorable you make things.

In the 1980s, scientists used lasers to make the most accurate measurement of the speed of light yet. It is 299,792,458 metres per second. This measurement will never be revised. If more accurate measurements are made in the future, it is the length of a metre that will change rather than the speed of light.

Try remembering the speed of light using one of the number tag systems. Draw each of the digits as you memorize them. Use a variety of colours and make each number and any image you wish to draw with it as big and exaggerated as possible. Sing each digit out loud as you draw it – this will be particularly effective if you are using the number rhyme tag system.

Come back to this tomorrow and see if you can still remember it. The chances are you will!

GET MOVING

Time: 60 minutes

By now you should be getting into the routine of your 60 minutes of exercise and you should be noticing the benefits of it. Ideally, you should aim to exercise three or four times a week. Try to get into the habit of exercising three or four times a week for 30 minutes between each weekly session.

This week, vary your routine a little bit more. For example, if you have been going swimming, try a few lengths in a stroke that you don't normally swim. If you haven't yet been swimming, is it an option you could explore today?

MENTAL CUSHION: RELAXATION

Time: 30 minutes

Last week you practised the Stretch and Relax routine on page 188. Spend another 30 minutes practising it again today.

Time: 5 minutes x 6

Every day for the rest of the week spend 5 minutes using one of the tag systems to remember one of the following. Each time you come back to the list, check to see if you can remember what you learned the day before. Try to remember some of the items on the list in the face of a distraction – such as the radio playing next to you – to help you hone your powers of concentration.

1. A telephone number in your address book
2. An important date in your diary that is happening in a month or two
3. A verse of a poem of your choice
4. All the items on your weekly shopping list
5. The names of three people you meet during the week
6. The date of birth of a friend or relative

Finally, can you still remember the speed of light?

Stay Sharp – Week 6

Time: 2 hours 15 minutes approximately
This week focuses on two areas of brain fitness, namely your logical and spatial skills.

THINKING LOGICALLY?

On the cards

Time: 3 minutes
Problem solving is always easier when it is presented to you in terms you can relate to. In the 1960s British psychologist Peter Wason (1924–2003) devised the four-card test to see how logically people think. Wason was an international chess master, and he wanted to challenge the idea that people are geared to working things out by pure logic. There are many variations on the four card test, all involving a set of four cards printed on both sides.

- Imagine a board-games maker has asked you to check that the cards in their game have been printed correctly. The cards are printed with squares and circles on one side and blue and red on the other. The rule is that if a card has a square on one side, then it is blue on the other side.
- You are given four of the cards – one showing a circle, one a square, one blue, one red. Which cards do you

need to turn over to find out if the rule has been broken?

- **Take your time to think this through carefully – and don't yet peek at the answer!**

The solution

Most people answer that you need to turn over the card with a square on it and the blue card. In fact, the answer is to turn over the square and the red. This is because the rule can be shown to be broken only if a card is found with a square on one side and red on the other. This solution goes so against our expectations that some people question if it is correct. Get some cards and try it for yourself.

Rather than concluding that those who get the answer wrong are simply unintelligent, Wason's theory was that as we go through life we learn to make short cuts in our logic to help us solve problems quickly. Although it works brilliantly most of the time, it breaks down when confronted with something that doesn't fit the pattern.

Breaking the rules

Time: 2 minutes

Interestingly many people find the kind of abstract problem posed by the Wason four-card set hard to solve yet find the test much easier if the same problem involves a more familiar situation.

- Imagine you are a policeman checking to see if there is any underage drinking in a bar. The rule is that if a person is drinking beer, then he must be over 18.
- When you come into the bar, you see four people: one is 16 and one is 20, one is drinking beer and one is drinking coke. Which drinkers do you need to check out to see if anyone is drinking under age?

The solution

This time the answer is easy to see: you check the 16-year-old to see what he is drinking, and you check the beer drinker to see how old he is. It is exactly the same problem as the cards above, yet now the answer is easy to grasp.

This is why it can be helpful to put a problem into a more familiar context if you are struggling to come up with the solution. Another way is to ask yourself what would somebody else, for example a builder, playwright or genius such as Leonardo da Vinci, do in this situation. Thinking outside the box will often help you come up with the answer.

A reliable witness?

Time: 3 minutes
Now try this test to see if your judgement is tricked when you think you are being completely logical. The task is to work out how reliable the witness is.

1. The facts: 80 per cent of the city's buses are red and 20 per cent are green.
2. The witness: although Stan Wright saw the bank robber get on a green bus, it was dark so he couldn't be absolutely sure.
3. When tested, 75 per cent of people correctly identify red and green buses in the dark.
4. What is the probability that the robber did get on a green bus?

The solution

Most people quickly conclude that the answer depends on the reliability of the witness and decide there was a 75 per cent chance of the robber's bus being green. This is, however, wrong. In actual fact, only 20 per cent of the buses are green, which means that it is more likely that the witness was wrong.

What is actually more important is that four out of five buses are red than that three out of four witnesses are reliable. Think about it like this. The witness is 75 per cent likely to correctly identify a green bus so the probability that the witness was right is 7.5 x 2, namely 15 per cent. However, it is 25 per cent likely that the witness was wrong and that the bus was red (80 per cent chance). This gives a slightly higher probability – a 2.5 x 8 or 20 per cent chance that the bus was red.

THINKING CRITICALLY

In recent years, some British universities have been promoting the idea of Thinking Skills Assessment to try and distinguish between otherwise similar candidates for entry. The basic approach of these tests was developed at the University of East Anglia's Centre for Research in Critical Thinking. Cambridge and other universities now often use Thinking Skills tests to help sort out the really clever students.

Rather than give students more learning, the idea of Thinking Skills is to encourage them to think clearly, logically and critically – examining the truth of statements, and identifying the flaws in arguments. Learning these skills can be a terrific way of developing the kind of superior judgement and thinking ability that you want to develop with age and experience. Here are a couple of examples of questions from the University of Cambridge's Critical Thinking tests for you to try.

The car challenge

Time: 3 minutes

The motor-car, which at first brought such freedom of private travel, has become a monster that is damaging our cities. Once motor-cars used to be affordable only by the rich – now there are 21 million cars in this country, and the number is still rising steeply. The huge number of cars in city centres has produced intolerable congestion and pollution. We have reached a stage where the use of private cars must be curbed. Otherwise, we will see a worsening of the current situation, where it is already becoming quicker to walk through a city in rush hour than to drive through it.

Which of the following best expresses the main conclusion of the argument above:

A. The motor car no longer gives us freedom of travel.
B. Increasing provision of public transport would solve traffic problems in city centres.
C. It is necessary to limit the use of motor cars by private individuals.
D. Pollution and congestion are damaging our city centres.
E. The number of people who can afford to own a motor-car has risen, and is continuing to rise.

Does Planet X exist?

Time: 3 minutes

Ever since Uranus was discovered in 1781, astronomers have thought there might be more planets to be discovered in the Solar System. Because of small deviations in the orbits of Uranus and Neptune – deviations which would occur if another planet existed – some astronomers think there must be another planet – Planet X. The search for Planet X is futile, because deviations would occur if the orbits had been wrongly predicted. Since Uranus and Neptune take many decades to circle the sun, astronomers must rely on old data in order to calculate their orbits. If this data is inaccurate, the calculated orbits are wrong. If the calculated orbits are wrong, Uranus and Neptune will deviate from them even if there is no Planet X.

Which of the following is the best statement of the flaw in the argument above?

A. From the fact that the old data is inaccurate, it cannot be inferred that the calculated orbits are wrong.

B. From the fact that the data about the orbits is old it cannot be inferred that it is inaccurate.

C. From the fact that deviations occur which would occur if Planet X existed, it cannot be inferred that Planet X exists.

D. From the fact that the calculated orbits are wrong, it cannot be inferred that Uranus and Neptune will deviate from them.

E. From the fact that Planet X has not been discovered, it cannot be inferred that the search for it is futile.

You can download many more of these to try on the University of Cambridge's Local Examinations Syndicate internet site: http://tsa.ucles.org.uk/downloads.html.

EPISODIC MEMORY REFRESHER

Time: 15 minutes

For the last couple of weeks you've had to spend time recalling three scenes from your past. This week try to remember all the details surrounding each of the questions below.

Find a quiet place where you can shut your eyes and take yourself back in time completely. Try to recall each scene in as much detail as possible, involving all of your senses. You may find it helpful to draw a Mind Map as you go along to help you explore each scene as fully as possible. Don't worry if your mind wanders: it will naturally take you down all kinds of interesting paths if you give it time. If you stray too far for too long, gently bring yourself back to the event in question and try to explore a different route. Spend 5 minutes on each question.

1. What was the bravest thing you did as a child?
2. What was your proudest moment?
3. What things did you pass on your route to junior school?

THINKING SPATIALLY

Time: 15 minutes

Your spatial skills are crucial to your confidence in navigating your way through the world around you. The next few exercises are designed to help you keep yours finely tuned.

Where's the point?

- **Shut your eyes and imagine different objects in the room around you. With your eyes still shut, point to different objects in turn as accurately as you can. Be ruthless in judging whether you got it!**
- **Practise this until you can be sure you get it right with every single object. Carry on until you can pinpoint at least 20 objects in the room.**

If you are finding this exercise tricky, try repeating it in reverse:

- **Keep your eyes wide open, choose an object and point at it. Now with your finger still pointing, shut your eyes. Try** to imagine as hard as you can exactly where your finger is pointing.

- **Open your eyes and check if you were right. If you were, close your eyes again with you finger still pointing in the right direction. Now drop your finger momentarily, then snap it back to the right direction.**
- **Open your eyes and check if you were right.**

Repeat this technique again and again, at home in your room and outside in the world – anywhere you can freely try pointing without someone calling the police!

GET MOVING

Time: 60 minutes

You should be familiar with this part of the plan. Spend the next 60 minutes on the exercise of your choice. If possible, try to choose a different exercise this week to the one you've chosen in previous weeks. Different exercises work different aspects of fitness. For example, if you have spent the last few weeks following a fitness DVD, could you get out on your bicycle today and go for an hour-long ride?

MENTAL CUSHION: RELAXATION

Time: 30 minutes

This week you are going to try a different exercise for relaxation. Go to a comfortable space where you won't be disturbed and follow the instructions for the meditation exercise on page 190 of Chapter 7.

TASK OF THE WEEK

Time: 5 minutes daily

Your task this week is to continue to fine-tune your spatial skills with this simple exercise.

1. Entirely in your imagination, try moving around your bathroom and brushing your teeth in as much detail as possible. Picture to yourself exactly where you will go, where different things are such as the taps and the toothpaste. This time shutting your eyes may actually help.

2. Once you've got the picture as complete in your mind's eye as you can get it, try acting it out where you are. Try it again and remember it in as much detail as you can.

3. Now, with that picture firmly in your mind, go to the bathroom, shut your eyes and try enacting the scene again. Touch the objects whenever appropriate to see how accurate your picture was.

4. Make adjustments if you remembered things out of place.

Once you have got the hang of this exercise, try it with another everyday task such as getting dressed or setting the table.

Stay Sharp – Week 7

Time: 3 hours 40 minutes approximately

Congratulations, you've reached the seventh and final week of your Stay Sharp Plan! This week, conclude the programme by further sharpening your powers of creativity, predominantly by using Mind Maps. Honing your creativity skills is an essential part of age-proofing your brain as it encourages greater mental elasticity. Keep working on your mental agility and you will keep your brain young and active.

Interestingly, because education systems tend to lean in favour of skills associated with left-brain thinking, many of us aren't very good at being as creative as we should be. All too often we get stuck on a particular way of thinking because our common sense or logic tells us that this is where a solution should be found. The key to coming up with amazing ideas is to also get the side of your brain involved that you use when you daydream. That way you engage your imagination, which as you should have observed by now, makes it much easier to achieve everything. Use both sides of your brain and you will come up with far more and far more impressive – ideas. However, what do we mean by the left and right sides of the brain?

A MARRIAGE OF TWO MINDS

Your brain is a marriage of two minds. Each half or hemisphere is a perfect mirror of the other, yet each works in subtly different ways. Like a husband and wife, they behave in their own special way, yet they are bound together by a bridge of fibres that enables them to exchange thoughts continually.

Back in the 1950s and 1960s, Roger Sperry and his team, together with Robert Ornstein, conducted a revealing series of experiments on the two halves of the brain. When students were asked to perform a series of mental tasks, including writing, drawing, listening to music, calculating and so on, the experiments showed that each half of the brain has its own preferred tasks. The right-brain tasks include spatial skills, colour, holistic thinking, daydreaming. The left-brain focus is on words, logic, numbers, lists and so on.

Left-brain strengths

Detail	Calculation
Logic	Facts
Language	Optimism
Analysis	

Right-brain strengths

Connections	Rhythm
Overview	Space and relationships
Daydreaming	Pessimism
Colour	Moody

MIND MAPS AND CREATIVITY

Time: 15 minutes

A Mind Map (see page 57) is a really effective creativity tool because it makes the most of your brain's synergetic way of working – drawing one engages both sides of it. If you regularly Mind Map you will help your brain to develop in this synergetic way and use it more efficiently.

You should by now feel really comfortable with Mind Mapping and have seen how it can help you generate ideas. In the earlier part of this programme, you were asked to Mind Map different uses for different objects, such as a penknife. Let's start this week with a similar exercise. As always, you will need plain paper and a selection of coloured pens.

Below is a random list of words. Your task is to think of as many uses of a plastic ruler in association with the word. Draw quick Mind Map sketches to help you and be as whacky and outrageous as you like. The uses don't have to be practical and the more ridiculous the better – laughter is a great stimulus to creativity.

1. Rock
2. Solar system
3. Architect's plan
4. Banana
5. Salt
6. Golf ball
7. Flag
8. Egg
9. Mountain
10. Napkin
11. Speech
12. Bus
13. Magazine
14. Coins
15. Rabbit
16. Hair

17. Juggling	22. Muscle
18. Hip	23. Fish
19. Elephant	24. France
20. Salad	25. Curb
21. Radio	

Suggestions

Here's some ideas I came up with in just a few minutes' brainstorming. If you can come up with better or more way out ideas, good for you; you're on the right track!

1. Rock – a plastic ruler could be used for scratching minerals and testing hardness. If you had a really huge plastic ruler you could use it to fire rock missiles over castle walls.
2. Solar system – a plastic ruler could be used for measuring the angle of objects in the night sky and identifying them. It could be used to hang a scale model of the solar system.
3. Architect's plan – a plastic ruler could be used to measure up drawings on a plan and for ensuring lines are straight. You could also smack it on the table to get everybody's attention when you present the plan.
4. Banana – the ruler could be used for deciding if the banana is straight enough according to government regulations! It could also be used for slicing the banana for a banana sandwich.
5. Salt – the ruler could be used for scraping the salt off the table after it has been spilled or used as a salt scoop to turn a fresh lake into a salt water one.

6. Golf ball – a plastic ruler could be used for lining up the ball perfectly for a green shot. If you taped lots of rulers together you could set up a Crazy Golf course on the green to play with.
7. Flag – taped together rulers can be used as a flag pole for flying the flag. You could also glue rulers around the edge of the flag to keep it stiff when the wind drops.
8. Egg – a ruler could be used for slicing the top off a boiled egg and cutting your toast into dipping soldiers.
9. Mountain – a ruler could be used for triangulating a mountain and working out its height. You could also use one as a make-shift tent pole when you camp out.
10. Napkin – a ruler could be used to fold the napkin round and for pressing the creases. You could also make a kite frame with rulers, attach the napkin and fly it at the top of a windy hill.
11. Speech – a ruler could be used as a pointer to indicate points on the display board. Alternatively, glue a few together to make a make-shift megaphone to speak through.
12. Bus – plastic rulers could be painted a bright neon colour and stuck as go-faster stripes to the side of the bus.
13. Magazine – if you can't find a telescope prop for a play, two rolled-up magazines mounted on a frame of plastic rulers should do the trick.
14. Coins – a plastic ruler could be used as a cue for playing shuv'penny football
15. Rabbit – a ruler could be used as a training stick when training rabbits to perform circus tricks.
16. Hair – a plastic ruler could be used to frizz hair into a fuzzy ball with static electricity.

17. Juggling – you could juggle plastic rulers instead of balls.
18. Hip – a plastic ruler could be used to gently tone the hips with slapping – or to make a walking frame if you slap yourself too hard!
19. Elephant – a plastic ruler could be used for reaching up to tickle an elephant behind its ears or scraping the mud off it when it's dirty.
20. Salad – a plastic ruler could be used for tossing a salad and slicing cucumber.
21. Radio – a plastic ruler could be used as a mount for a personal radio.
22. Muscle – You could mount two lumps of iron on to reinforced plastic rulers to make a makeshift dumbbell – then use another ruler to check that your muscles are growing in size.
23. Fish – plastic rulers could be taped together as a fishing rod, then used to measure the size of the one that got away.
24. France – a plastic ruler could be used as the starting point for a discussion on the coming of the French Revolution and the origins of the metre.
25. Curb – a plastic ruler could be used to build up collapsed or missing curbs.

Although just a game, the plastic ruler exercise is a game with real value; it plays with your imagination. Games like these help you stimulate the kind of connections that unlock some of the creative potential of your brain. Using Mind Maps, exercises like these increase your ability to make associations and create images.

WHERE'S YOUR DREAM HOLIDAY?

Time: 20 minutes

This time, draw a Mind Map of what would be for you the holiday of a life-time.

Start with an image at the centre that represents the core of the holiday – the location, you and the person you wish to take with you, a suitcase. Anything that seems appropriate to you. Then add main branches and sub-branches with ideas of what the holiday would involve. Keep asking yourself questions as you go along – where would you like to go? How will you get there? What you would like to do? How will it make you feel? How long do you want to go? When do you plan to leave? Why do you want to go? If you are still a hot-house of ideas after the 20 minutes is up, keep going until you are satisfied.

FIRST AND LAST

Time: 4 minutes

In The 7-Day Get Sharp Plan you were given the first and last lines of a story and asked to fill in the gap of what happened in between. As before, plunge straight into the exercise and let your imagination fuel your story. Give yourself no more than 2 minutes.

'Once upon a time there was a badger who was born with feathers on his paws …
… And he vowed to change the washer immediately if the tap decided to drip again.'

CREATIVITY TIPS

Often the biggest obstacle to creativity is the censorship your logical left brain imposes on your right. Whenever your right brain comes up with an idea, your left brain stops it in its tracks, saying 'That just won't work', 'Come on, be serious', 'That's disgusting', 'No one will let you get away with that', and so on.

Your left brain is great for turning vague ideas into reality. To really get your creativity going, you need both halves of your brain to work together. Most of us probably need help to encourage the freedom of your right brain to play.

Keep these tips in mind to help you keep your creative juices flowing. Even better, sum them up on a Mind Map to remember them and post it on your fridge for a few days:

1. **Exaggerate**
2. **Be humorous**
3. **Use your senses to stimulate ideas**
4. **Use colour**
5. **Use rhythm and music**
6. **Use images**
7. **Move quickly**
8. **Allow yourself to get excited**
9. **Think positively**
10. **Take regular breaks**
11. **Use Mind Maps**

Now spin a story around these lines, again giving yourself
2 minutes to complete the story:

'Toby had always known that his grandmother's spider plants
were evil ...
... the peach was soft and the ice cream extinguished the
dragon's burning fire.'

EPISODIC MEMORY REFRESHER

Time: 15 minutes

Over the last few weeks you've had to try to recall three
scenes from your past. For this last week try to recall all
the details surrounding each of the questions below.

As before, find a quiet place where you can shut your
eyes and take yourself back in time completely. Try to
recall each scene in as much detail as possible, involving
all of your senses. You may find it helpful to draw a Mind
Map as you go along to help you explore each scene as
fully as possible. Don't worry if your mind wanders: it will
naturally take you down all kinds of interesting paths if
you give it time. If you stray too far for too long, gently
bring yourself back to the event in question and try
to explore a different route. Spend 5 minutes on each
question.

1. What was the first film or theatre show you ever went to see?
2. What was the most exciting day of your childhood?
3. What did your mum's kitchen smell like in the morning
   before you went to school?

PRACTISE YOUR SKILL

Time: 30 minutes

In The 7-Day Get Sharp Plan you had to practise a skill of your choice for 15 minutes a day. Return to that skill now and spend 30 minutes playing with it.

COMPLETE THE POEM

Time: 25 minutes

Writing prose or poetry is a fantastic way to get your mental juices flowing, especially if you inject as much humour into it as possible.

Today you're going to compose limericks, a traditionally comic form of poetry. First of all, read through the two limericks below to remind yourself of the way in which a limerick scans:

> There was a young lady of Niger
> Who smiled as she rode on a tiger;
> They returned from the ride
> With the lady inside,
> And the smile on the face of the tiger.
> *William Cosmo Monkhouse*

There was a young lady whose chin,
Resembled the point of a pin;
So she had it made sharp,
And purchased a harp,
And played several tunes with her chin.
Edward Lear

As you can see, a limerick is only five lines long. Lines 1, 2 and 5 have seven to ten syllables and rhyme with one another; lines 3 and 4 have five to seven syllables and also rhyme with each other.

Now complete the following limericks, spending no more than 5 minutes on each. Have as much fun with them as you can – be as silly or as rude as you wish!

1. There was a young otter called Sam …
2. A crusty old man with a spade …
3. There was a fat baker called Brown …
4. A man who was incredibly rich …
5. There was a young lady from Woking …

RECLAIM THE ARTIST WITHIN!

Time: 20 minutes

Many people give up drawing soon after leaving school since they have neither the confidence nor the time to develop their artistic abilities. No matter how good – or bad – you think you are, your brain will always benefit from anything you try to draw, whether it is a simple doodle or a full-blown picture.

Perhaps without noticing, you have been exercising your artistic talent throughout the programme, since every time you draw a Mind Map you are in fact drawing a picture of words, image and colour.

Another way to exercise your artistic talents is to practise doodling with your non-writing hand. Although the results may not be quite up to Monet's standards, the exercise it gives to your brain will more than make up for that.

Spend 10 minutes now doodling with your non-writing hand. Draw anything you like, be it lines, spirals, shapes, people, letters – you name it, anything you like. Just let your mind wander with your pen or pencil and see what happens.

The next part of this exercise is to find an object that you like the look of and copy it, this time using your normal writing hand. Use a pencil, pens, or paint as you prefer. Don't judge yourself and listen to your inner monologue about how good or bad you think it is, simply focus on the task at hand and enjoy the liberation of being so absorbed.

If you really enjoy yourself and wish to carry on beyond the 10 minutes, do. You could also consider developing your artistic skills further with regular practise or by joining an art class.

Even if you don't enjoy drawing, try to get into the habit of doodling. When you doodle you allow your brain to daydream – and it's when you daydream that you can come up with some truly amazing ideas and solutions.

GET MOVING

Time: 60 minutes

The fact this might be the last week of your 60-minute Get Moving sessions shouldn't mean the end of your regular physical workouts. As you exercise today, observe how much progress you have made since you started The 7-Week Stay Sharp Plan. How much easier is it to complete your routine? Are you able to achieve more? How much fitter and stronger do you feel? Use your positive observations to motivate yourself to exercise regularly.

MENTAL CUSHION: RELAXATION

Time: 30 minutes

Last week you practised a meditation technique at the end of the session. Spend another 30 minutes on it today (see page 190 for instructions).

TASK OF THE WEEK

Time: 10 minutes daily and 30 minutes

You have two final tasks this week, the first a Mind Mapping task, the second a doodling one.

1. **Set aside 10 minutes every day to doodle in a notepad, spending 5 minutes with your non-writing hand and another 5 with your writing hand.**
2. **Draw two Mind Maps, the first to identify a problem in your life, and the second to brainstorm how you can resolve it. Spend 10 minutes on the first Mind Map and 20 minutes on the second.**

TIPS: Be relaxed and whacky, and follow up the associations and implications of each problem or solution in as free and easy a fashion as you can. The more extreme your ideas are the better. Never let your mind censor ideas because they won't work or they are too outrageous or shocking.

Conclusion

Now you've got it, keep it

Congratulations! Now that you've reached the end of The 7-Week Stay Sharp Plan you should be feeling as mentally fit as you were 10 years ago – if not more! In order to maintain and build on your new-found mental agility, you need to keep on challenging and stimulating that amazing brain of yours. Before we look at how you can do this, let's return to the self-assessment questionnaires to get the full measure of the progress you have made.

How much progress have you made?

PART ONE – HOW SHARP HAVE YOU BECOME?

Once again, give yourself a score on a scale of 1 (easy) to 5 (real problem) for how easy you find it to remember these things:

Remembering names

- [ ] Someone you've just met
- [ ] Friends
- [ ] Family members
- [ ] Places such as restaurants you've visited
- [ ] Titles of books and movies you've seen

Remembering numbers

- [ ] PIN number
- [ ] Bank account number
- [ ] Familiar phone numbers
- [ ] New phone numbers
- [ ] Doing simple sums

Remembering dates

- [ ] Birthdays and anniversaries
- [ ] Appointments
- [ ] Household chores

Remembering where

- [ ] Where you put things (keys, remote controls, etc)
- [ ] Where you parked the car
- [ ] Directions

Remembering stories

- [ ] What you watched on TV last night, read in the papers, etc
- [ ] What you were just saying
- [ ] What the other person was just saying
- [ ] The right word for it

Age-proof Your Brain

Add up your scores, and then see how you did:

20–30 Congratulations! You have no memory problems whatsoever and have made superb progress. Follow the maintenance plan to keep your brain in tip-top condition.

31–40 You're doing extremely well and have come on in leaps and bounds! Keep looking for new ways to challenge your brain and make sure you stick with the maintenance plan in this chapter to eradicate the last of your mild memory problems.

41–60 Pretty good! You are still experiencing some memory problems and should go back over the quick-win techniques in Chapter 3 to make sure you are giving your brain the best possible chance to perform for you. Make sure you follow the maintenance plan.

61–80 You're making progress! You need to persevere with the programme as you still have moderate difficulty remembering things. Study the quick-win techniques in Chapter 3 to make sure that you have grasped the different ways that the memory techniques can help you. For example, if you are still struggling to remember the names of people you meet, make sure you are using the techniques recommended on page 72 to link their name to their face. Also, go back to the detailed questionnaire on pages 201–210 of Chapter 8 to identify any influences in your lifestyle that may be jeopardizing your progress. Repeat The 7-Day Get Sharp Plan and take this test again. If your score is 60 or under, move on to the maintenance plan. If not, repeat The 7-Week Stay Sharp Plan and return to this questionnaire to assess the progress you make.

81–100 You're still struggling to improve your performance and are experiencing severe memory problems. Go back to the detailed questionnaire on pages 201–210 of Chapter 8 to identify any influences in your lifestyle that may be jeopardizing your progress. You should also consider consulting your doctor as there may be a social or health issue that is consistently interfering with your performance. Return to the quick-win techniques in Chapter 3 to make sure that you have grasped the different ways that the memory techniques can help you. For example, if you still have problems remembering PIN numbers, make sure you are using one of the number tag systems to help you learn them. Work your way through the entire programme again, starting with The 7-Week Stay Sharp Plan. Keep persevering and you will start to see a marked improvement in your performance.

PART TWO – THE 7-MINUTE MIND MAKEOVER

As in the Introduction, this part of your personal assessment is designed to challenge your mental performance in six different areas:

Short-term memory	Logic
Long-term memory	Analysis
Language	Creativity

All you need is seven minutes of your time, paper, a pen or pencil and something to accurately time yourself with (most mobile phones have a built-in stopwatch). Follow the instructions carefully – make sure you only give yourself the amount of time specified for each question – then check the answers at the back of the book to see how well you did.

MEMORY TONER

Time: 60 seconds
Focus: Short-term memory

Number punching

Below are series of numbers. The challenge is to remember as many as you can in just 60 seconds.

Cover up the numbers, leaving just the top number of the left column exposed. Memorize it, cover it up and write it down. (Use your writing hand to cover the number to avoid the temptation of simply writing what you see.) Now reveal the second number. Remember it, cover it up and write it down. Go down through the list for 60 seconds, getting as far as you can.

At the end of the 60 seconds, check your answers. How many did you get right? Give yourself one point for each number you correctly remembered.

2345	346789259
7734	946358905
32567	7468317945
680246	3410667326
326789	88763289539
2547881	45722689438
7802654	993479098685
10191485	591742007360
54714853	198567457326

SCORE /18

MEMORY BUILDER

Time: 60 seconds
Focus: Long-term memory

Fact bank

Here is a list of seven names. Give yourself 20 seconds to remember them. Cover up the book then write down all the names you can remember. Give yourself one point for each name you remember and a bonus point if you remember them all.

George	Boris
Jonah	Mike
Selina	Caroline
Sarah	

SCORE: /8

Here is a list of ingredients needed to make a recipe. Give yourself 40 seconds to remember them, and then cover up the book to write them down in the correct order. Give yourself half a point for each ingredient and half a point for each quantity you remember. If you remember everything in the correct order give yourself an extra bonus point.

75g Muscovado sugar
40g unsalted butter
1 egg
2 medium ripe bananas
½ apple
SCORE: /10

125g self-raising flour
½ tsp nutmeg
½ tsp cinnamon
Pinch of Salt

WORD POWER

Time: 60 seconds
Focus: Language

Anagram
Give yourself 60 seconds to solve the transport anagrams below. The first letters of each should spell out the name of something they all have in common. Give yourself 2 points for each anagram you solve and 2 bonus points for the extra name.

ËCRNOIT
HLAAP MROOE
SCORE: /10

LNRATUE
AABS

LOGIC BOOSTER

Time: 60 seconds
Focus: Logic skills

Tall story
Sam is 14 inches taller than Mary. The difference between Sam and Richard is 2 inches less than between Richard and Mary. Sam at 6 foot 6 inches is the tallest. How tall are Richard and Mary? Award yourself 4 points per height correctly answered.
    SCORE: /8

ANALYTIC POWER

Time: 60 seconds
Focus: Logic skills

Codebreaker
Can you spot the hidden message in this text message, apparently on a business matter, from a personal assistant to her lover? Give yourself 6 points if you correctly decipher the message.

    Meet Mr Smith at noon. The mine reopens at 7pm.
    SCORE: /6

CREATIVE THINKING

Time: 120 seconds
Focus: Logic skills

Making connections
Give yourself 120 seconds to brainstorm as many different uses for a sock as you can by linking the sock to the following list of words. Be as imaginative and ridiculous as you like!

Telephone	Superglue
Christmas tree	Anchovies
Breakfast	Hand cream
Peacock	Calculator
Apple	Raisin
Jupiter	Tipex
Zebra	Rain
Singapore	Dictionary
Banana	Chimney
Pencil	Smoke alarm

Score yourself according to how many uses you came up with:

0–10 uses	2 points
11–20 uses	4 points
21–30 uses	6 points
31–40 uses	8 points
40+ uses	10 points
SCORE: /10	

Add up your scores, and then see how you did:

60–70 Fabulous! You are now sharp as a tack! Make sure you keep that fabulous brain of yours in mint condition by following the maintenance programme in this chapter. You need to keep exercising your brain to keep it in shape.

45–59 Your brain is now pretty fit although you need to make sure that you keep on stretching yourself. Make sure you follow the maintenance programme in this chapter to help you keep up the good work.

30–44 Although this is quite a good score, you should aim to get to the next level. Make sure you are using the quick-win techniques in Chapter 3 as these will all help you boost your performance.

15–29 Your brain is still quite out of shape and there is definite room for improvement. Return to the quick-win techniques in Chapter 3 to make sure that you have understood how the techniques can help you and make sure you get into the habit of using them. Repeat The 7-Day Get Sharp Plan, making a conscious effort to use as many of the quick-win techniques as possible. Stick with the programme as you will be able to turn round your mental fitness.

0–14 Although your score is disappointing, don't be disheartened. Return to the quick-win techniques in Chapter 3 as you may not have fully grasped them and how they can help you. Spend some time practising the techniques until they become second nature. Repeat The 7-Day Get Sharp Plan and The 7-Week Stay Sharp Plan, making a conscious effort to use as many of the quick-win techniques as possible. Both of these plans are designed to help you turn round your mental performance and if you persevere with them you will be able to get your brain back into shape.

Next compare your scores from the two parts of the self-assessment with the results you achieved first time around in the Introduction. Are you doing better overall? In which areas have you made the most progress? Are there still any areas that need work? If you are still under-performing in one area, make sure that you focus on this area as part of your on-going maintenance plan.

YOUR BODY HAS AN AVERAGE AGE OF 15 AND A HALF!

Whatever age you are at the moment, don't be deceived by that number! According to Jonas Frisen, a neurologist at the Karolinska Institute in Stockholm, Sweden, the average age of your body is actually about 15 and a half.

It has long been believed that the body completely renews itself every seven years and there is now evidence to back up this theory. Frisen has developed a method testing the extent of carbon 14 in cell DNA to measure accurately the age of body tissue. He has discovered that the age of different parts of your body varies enormously. For example, your gut (excluding the lining) is about 15.9 years old, your bones around 10 years, your skin just over 2 weeks and your gut lining a modest 5 days. The only parts of the body that appear to be about the same age as your birth age – at least on present evidence – are the neurons of the cerebral cortex in your brain, the muscle cells of your heart and the inner lens cells of your eyes.

If your body is able to renew itself, why then does it experience the physical effects of ageing? The answer lies in your mitochondrial DNA. This is the DNA found in mitochondria, miniature cell bodies that convert food molecules into energy. It's this DNA that mutates and deteriorates the most quickly over time – and makes it hard for cells to renew themselves as accurately. Scientists are now trying to develop a method of protecting or repairing our mitochondrial DNA. If they succeed in their mission, the implications for the onset of age are enormous. Your body would remain as young and fit as your renewed cells. The only thing that age would bring would be wisdom and experience.

Now you've got it, keep it

Everything you have been doing over the last eight weeks has been designed to exercise your brain, encourage it to build new connections and to work more efficiently for you. You should be finding it much easier to memorize whatever you wish to remember and be taking far more interest in everything going on around you. This will be especially true if you have adopted a more playful attitude to learning and living: your brain loves to have fun with the information and experiences it is exposed to and will perform much better if it has the freedom to be as imaginative as possible. This is how the most innovative ideas are generated.

You should also be feeling more alert and energized, especially if you have been able to stick to the exercise, diet and relaxation recommendations in this book. To illustrate this, consider for a moment a world class Formula One racing car that is propelled to incredible speeds by its engine. Without a strong, sleek, properly fuelled body, it hasn't a hope of setting a new world record, let alone winning a race. Look after your body and you will give your brain the best possible chance to win your races.

How can you build on all of the progress you have made? In short, keep your mind challenged and your body properly exercised and nourished.

Daily

Get into the habit of looking for different ways to stimulate your brain on a daily basis:

1. **Play games with your mind as you go about your daily life to keep it stimulated. For example, when you do your weekly shop, instead of writing a straightforward list,**

draw a quick Mind Map. Give yourself 5 minutes to memorize everything on it then go shopping without it (or fold it up and don't look at it again until you are ready to go to the checkout).

2. Try to do one thing differently every day, whether it is tying your shoe laces left-handed rather than right-handed, cooking a new recipe or walking a slightly different route to a regular destination. This will reduce your brain's tendency to carry out familiar tasks on autopilot.

3. Get some fresh air everyday and spend a couple of minutes deep breathing to help keep you relaxed, focused and refreshed.

4. Make sure that you use at least one of the quick-win techniques every day (see Chapter 3). These are your core brain tools and they will help your mind perform at its best for you.

Weekly

1. Once or twice a week, spend 7 minutes giving yourself an intensive 7-Minute Mind Makeover. There are a few in the Appendix to get you started. After you have completed them, either adapt them to create new ones or simply spend 7 minutes on a mentally challenging exercise of your choice, such as a cryptic crossword, a couple of brain teasers or logic puzzles (there are plenty to be found on the Internet or in puzzle books).

2. Make a point of learning something new every week, whether it is information in a book or newspaper article you read or in a documentary you see on television.

Make a note of what it is and test yourself on it the following week.

3. Exercise for 30–60 minutes at least three times every week.
4. Set aside 15–30 minutes to enjoy one of the relaxation exercises in Chapter 7.

Once a year

1. Return to the brain fitness questionnaires to assess your overall mental agility. If your score is the same or better, simply carry on with the daily and weekly maintenance plan. If it has declined, return to The 7-Week Stay Sharp Plan in Chapter 8 and work through it again to boost your performance.
2. Take up a brand new interest or hobby, for example try learning a new language or musical instrument, and stick with it for at least three months.

Stick to this maintenance plan and you should be able to age-proof your brain indefinitely. Even better, you should also retain an energy and vigour for life that will be the envy of your contemporaries and also of people half your age. With your agile mind, infinite experience and 15-and-a-half-year-old body you are and will remain a formidable force for the future.

Appendix

More 7-Minute Mind Makeovers

Below is a structure that you can work to in order to keep up your weekly 7-Minute Mind Makeovers. You will need to start sourcing new material for some of the sections once you have worked your way through them.

As before, The 7-Minute Mind Makeovers should boost your mental performance in six areas:

Short-term memory   Logic
Long-term memory   Analysis
Language   Creativity

Remember to resist the temptation to cheat! Never allow yourself a little longer over the routine or to bend the rules, even a little. They are only short exercises and being disciplined really pays off. As before, you need to time yourself accurately with a stopwatch. You'll also need a pen or pencil, paper and two die.

Short-term memory

Time: 60 seconds

Remember three numbers and names in your address book – you never know when you might lose it. Before you start, refresh your memory of all the numbers you've learned on previous days.

Long-term memory

Time: 60 seconds

Learn the ingredients of one of your favourite recipes using the number tags technique (see page 66). Buy the ingredients without using a shopping list and make it for supper within the next three days.

Language

Time: 60 seconds

Choose one word from the following word list and use the letters to make as many more words of at least three letters as you can:

Fortunate	Atmospheric
Rebuking	Halitosis
Merchandise	Stimulation
Lubricant	Gerrymander
Antiaircraft	Desertification
Butterfly	Stratosphere
Icelandic	Respectable

Workaholic	Metropolitan
Deadline	Topicality
Preternatural	Starvation
Fragmented	Succulent
Daffodil	Rhythmically
Carnival	Blackcurrant
Freightliner	Barnstorming
Trickster	Shambolically

Once you've used up all these words, find your own letters by taking 10 letters at random from a Scrabble set.

LOGIC

Time: 120 seconds

Solve the following visual logic problems:

Week 1

Two trains are on a head-on collision course. The trains are currently 65 miles apart. The northbound train is travelling at 55 miles per hour and the southbound train is travelling at 80 miles per hour. What will be the distance between the two trains two minutes before they collide?

Week 2

Several cartons of chocolate bars are being shipped from a manufacturer to warehouses where they will be prepackaged to sell to stores. The number of chocolate bars in each carton needs to be equally divided among 3, 4, 5, or

7 stores. What is the least number of bars that each carton should contain?

Week 3

Students at Kings School with a class size of under 30 took a maths test. One third of the class got a grade B, one quarter a B–, one sixth a C and one eighth of them failed. The remainder of the students got a grade A. How many students got an A?

Week 4

Mike loves dumplings. He can eat 32 of them in an hour. His brother Luke needs 3 hours to eat the same amount. How long will it take them both together to eat 32 dumplings?

ANALYSIS

Time: 60 seconds

Practise your ability to scan quickly and spot patterns by opening a page in this book at random and seeing how many times you can spot the pair of letters 'er' appearing on this page and the following pages in the allotted time.

CREATIVITY

Time: 60 seconds

Throw two dice (one after the other) to select four words at random from the 'Objects' list, and one from the 'Hero' list. Then weave a story or picture from the five words in two minutes:

Objects

1	1	Rotweiler	4	1	Sex
1	2	Castle	4	2	Wizard
1	3	Hill	4	3	Instant coffee
1	4	Cup	4	4	Hermit
1	5	Invisible	4	5	Kalashnikov
1	6	Pizza	4	6	Painting
2	1	Train	5	1	Rubber
2	2	Demolition	5	2	Crumpet
2	3	Whale	5	3	Cow
2	4	Waterway	5	4	Blue cheese
2	5	Girl	5	5	Enchantment
2	6	Rabbit	5	6	Internet
3	1	Hump	6	1	Used car
3	2	Brushstroke	6	2	French
3	3	iPod	6	3	Wings
3	4	Desert	6	4	Hell
3	5	Angel	6	5	Outer space
3	6	Beauty	6	6	Cloudburst

Hero

1	1	Alice	2	4	Salome
1	2	Aisha	2	5	Josef Stalin
1	3	Katya	2	6	Dracula
1	4	The Gorgon	3	1	The emperor
1	5	Flash Gordon	3	2	The little flower seller
1	6	Tony Blair	3	3	Harvey
2	1	Marylin Monroe	3	4	Godzilla
2	2	Rumpelstiltskin	3	5	Harry Potter
2	3	The Kraken	3	6	Brian

4	1 Alhazen	5	4 Julia
4	2 Mae West	5	5 Mrs Fordworthy
4	3 Saddam Hussein	5	6 Rub-a-dub-dub
4	4 Spiderman	6	1 Aladdin
4	5 Hannibal Lector	6	2 Persephone
4	6 The shining girl	6	3 Mephistopheles
5	1 David	6	4 Bill Gates
5	2 Rupert	6	5 Condoleeza Rice
5	3 The wall	6	6 Beyoncé

Be as absurd and outrageous as you like. Try to make sure your story has a beginning, a middle and an end, structuring it like this:

- **Once upon a time ... (set-up the scenario)**
- **So ... (explore the consequences)**
- **And then ... (wrap it up).**

Answers

Introduction

Word Power, page 7
Anagram: STEM, Citrus, Apricot, Grape, Plum

Logic Booster, page 8
Age-old logic: George is 15, Tony is 9 and John is 24.

You can work it out like this:

1) We are told that the three friends' ages add up to 48. You can write this in algebra form:

G + T + J = 48

2) We are also told that George and Tony's ages together equal John's. You can write this in algebra form too:

G + T = J

From this we can see that 2 x J = 48
Therefore John must be 24 years old.

3) We are told that in six years' time, John will be twice Tony's age, or Tony will be half John's age. You can write this in algebra form:

$$T + 6 = (J+6)/ 2$$

Since you know John is 24, you can substitute this in the equation:

$$T + 6 = (24+6)/ 2 = 15$$

Therefore $T = 15 - 6 = 9$
Therefore Tony is 9 years old.

4) Going back to equation one:

$$G = 48 - J - T$$

Therefore $G = 48 - 24 - 9 = 15$
Therefore George is 15.

TIP: Try using algebra to help you.

Analytic Power, page 8
Codebreaker: The hidden message is, 'Tonight Yours, Darling' spelled out by the first letters of each word.

Chapter 4

Word Power, page 87
Phrase round the edge:

1. Mixed race
2. Cash on delivery
3. Just in time
4. Taking half measures
5. A game of two halves
6. I'm over the moon

Logic Booster, page 88

Age-old logic: I'm 30

If my age is T and my mother's age is M, the relationship between our current ages can be expressed as:

$$\text{(my age) } T = \frac{M}{2} \text{ (half my mother's age)}$$

The relationship between our ages 15 years ago can be expressed as:

$$\text{(my age fifteen years ago) } T - 15 = \frac{M - 15}{3} \text{ (a third of my}$$
mother's age fifteen years ago)

To work out my age T, we need an equation with just the unknown T. We therefore need to find an alternative way to express the other unknown M. Another way to express M in the first equation is $M = 2T$.

Therefore we can substitute $2T$ in for M in the second equation:

$$T - 15 = \frac{2T - 15}{3}$$

With just the unknown of T, we can calculate T.

$$3 \times (T - 15) = \frac{2T - 15}{3} \times 3$$
$$3T - 45 = 2T - 15$$
$$3T - 2T = 45 - 15$$
$$T = 30$$

Therefore my age (T) is 30.

Analytic Power, page 88

Odd one out: Mummy – all the other words begin and end with the same letter.

Skill Developing, page 90

Music test:

1. Blue Danube
2. Yesterday
3. Scarborough Fair
4. Danny Boy

Brain Stretcher Quiz, page 91

1. The Beatles
2. Amazon
3. Michelangelo
4. Daniel Radcliffe
5. Bucharest
6. Cambodia
7. Chest
8. Istanbul
9. Tower of London
10. Emily Davison
11. *Great Expectations*
12. Photon
13. Anne Brontë
14. Jackson
15. Personal Digital Assistant
16. Gastropod
17. St Petersburg
18. Anne Frank
19. Angel Falls
20. Magnetic Resonance Imaging
21. Hematite
22. Lines of equal pressure
23. Titan
24. Pompeii
25. Arthur Miller
26. Wal-Mart
27. Enola Gay
28. Kilimanjaro
29. Materazzi
30. Virginia Woolf
31. Cyrus the Great
32. Hippocampus
33. Jurassic
34. Weser
35. Ether
36. Dushanbe
37. UNESCO
38. Black Eyed Peas
39. *The Tempest*
40. Sarajevo

41. The movement of a galaxy
42. Lavoisier
43. Red
44. Sequoiadendron
    giganteum (Giant sequoia)
45. On the Moon

Word Power, page 106
Word ladders:
1. WARM – WARD – CARD – CORD – COLD
2. GIVE – LIVE – LIKE – LAKE – TAKE
3. GRASS – CRASS – CRESS – TRESS – TREES

Logic Booster, page 107
Seating arrangements: Julia on Robin's right in the front row; Paul is sitting behind him in the second row; George is in the third row; Susan and David are sitting in the fourth row in a line behind Julia and Robin.

Analytic Power, page 108
Three house, three needs: This classic puzzle has no solution in 2D. You can solve it by placing the items on a bagel or doughnut shape in 3D. In the picture below, E (electricity) is linked to house 3 by going over the top and re-entering through the hole in the middle.

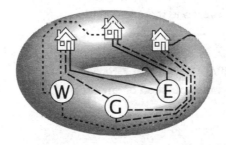

Skill Developing, page 110

Music test:

1.   Moon River
2.   Summertime
3.   Don't Cry for Me, Argentina

Word Power, page 114

Crossed love:

It's better to have loved and lost
than to have never loved at all.
Alfred, Lord Tennyson

Love is not love
that alters when it alteration finds
William Shakespeare

She walks in beauty,
Like the night of cloudless climes and starry skies;
Lord Byron

How do I love thee? Let me count the ways.
Elizabeth Barrett Browning

Shall I compare thee to a summer's day?
Thou art more lovely and more temperate:
William Shakespeare

I have spread my dreams under your feet;
Tread softly because you tread on my dreams.
W B Yeats

O, my luve is like a red, red rose,
That's newly sprung in June.
Robert Burns

Logic Booster, page 115

Food for thought:

1. 63 kg. (1 per cent of 75 is 0.75. She wants to end up at 84 per cent weight. The answer is 0.75 x 84.)

2. £52.50. (If it costs him £45 to feed his chickens for 9 days, it costs him £5 a day to feed 100 chickens. To feed 150 chickens for a day would therefore cost him £7.50. To feed them for a week would cost £7.50 times 7.)

3. 200 grams. (You've got 12 kg to last 10 days, so you've got just 1.2 kg for all the dogs' meals each day. Since there are six dogs, each portion is 1.2 kg divided by 6, which is 0.2 kg or 200 grams.)

Analytic Power, page 116

Morese code: What God hath wrought

Skill Developing, page 118

Music test:

1. Jerusalem
2. Auld Lang Syne

3. Happy Birthday
4. EC

Logic Booster, page 124

Cruel Christmas:

1. Courvoisier runs up the path on virgin snow; there are no footprints, therefore Hubert cannot have just arrived.
2. Although the gun is smoking, Madame Hubert's blood has already congealed. She must have been shot some time before.
3. When Courvoisier asks Hubert to step aside, his feet should leave two damp marks of melting snow if he has indeed just come in; the floor is clearly dry.

Analytic Power, page 125

Morse code: Memories are made of this

Logic Booster, page 131

The runaway pony:

1. The young lady is well built and well groomed whereas the pony is small and a little scruffy.
2. The lady does not check the girth before mounting nor does she use the stirrups which presumably would be too short for her.
3. The boy's first reaction is to check if his pony is sound.

Analytic Power, page 132

Morse code: Anything is possible

Chapter 8

Chunking, page 214

You could arrange the words into the following three groups: beauty, food and office.

Memory Toner, page 227

A reliable witness 1:

1. A pink coat.
2. She didn't come out of the grocers. When she came out of the newsagents she had a wallet and some coins in her hand.
3. You didn't see.
4. A hoodie.
5. Yes, the hood was down.
6. Neither. He was short.
7. He grabbed the girl's arm in one hand and her phone in the other.
8. You didn't see. All you saw was that he grabbed the girl's left arm.

Memory Toner, page 228

A reliable witness 2:

1. Blue
2. From north to south
3. The man on the pavement
4. The left or east side
5. The small black dog
6. The left or east side
7. A man
8. The newsagents

Memory Toner, page 235

Recognition quiz:

1. Jane Fonda
2. Lake Superior
3. Mary Anne Evans
4. Stepson
5. Tashkent
6. By lightning strikes
7. Gluteus maximus
8. Yenisey-Angara
9. Iran
10. Antonio Banderas
11. Boreas
12. Sirius (this only appears to be the brightest star; Deneb is many times brighter, looking dimmer because it is so far away)

13. Cork
14. $10,000
15. St Petersburg
16. Osmonds
17. *The Adventures of Tom Sawyer*
18. *Emma*
19. New Guinea
20. An alignment of planets
21. Guanine
22. 2004
23. Alicia Keys
24. K2
25. In an ancient parchment
26. Saint Augustine
27. Chinese giant salamanders
28. 1,227.98 km/h
29. 120 years 237 days
30. Hydrogen
31. Jalal Talabani
32. Corpus callosum
33. Cherry brandy
34. Wild garlic
35. Hungarian
36. Den Xaoping
37. Edward Barton
38. Mark Philippoussis
39. *As You Like It*
40. 5 per cent
41. Hartsfield, Atlanta
42. Harriet Beecher Stowe
43. 13.7 billion years
44. US dollar
45. John D Rockefeller

Recall, page 245

1. Ferdinand Magellan
2. Howard Shore
3. 'I faced it all and I stood tall; And did it my way.'
4. In the Crown Jewels in the Tower of London
5. Chinese Emperor Qin Shi Huang
6. Vladimir Ulyanov
7. Agra in India
8. Whale shark
9. 299,792 (300,000 will do)
10. Inventing the transistor
11. Basil, parmesan cheese, olive oil, pine nuts and garlic
12. Liverpool
13. The tongue of a snail
14. Jupiter
15. Woody Allen
16. Hugo Chávez
17. Mont Blanc

18. Jean-Paul Sartre
19. Colombia
20. Michael Collins
21. Michael Collins
22. 2240
23. Bears
24. Milan
25. Russia

26. Tim Burton
27. Jose Manuel Barroso
28. Gold, Tin, Zinc, Krypton
29. Radius, Ulna, Scapula, Humerus
30. A. Madhya Pradesh
    B. Alaska

Thinking Critically, page 287
The car challenge: C
Does Planet X exist?: B

Conclusion

Word Power, page 313
Anagram: CARS, Citroën, Alpha Romeo, Renault, Saab

Logic Booster, page 314
Tall story: If Sam is 6 foot 6 inches tall, Mary must be 5 foot 4 inches tall, and Richard 6 foot. This is because Richard is 6 inches shorter than Sam and 8 inches taller than Mary.

Analytic Power, page 314
Codebreaker: The hidden message is, 'Meet at mine 7pm' using every third word of the message (starting with 'Meet').

Appendix

Logic, page 325

Week 1: The trains will be 4.5 miles apart. If the trains are moving toward each other you need to combine their speeds to get their speed basis, i.e. 55 + 80 = 135mph. Next divide this speed by 60 minutes to give the speed they are travelling at per minute, namely 2.25 miles/minute. Multiply this by two to work out the distance apart they will be at 2 minutes before impact.

Week 2: There should be 420 chocolate bars in each carton. This is because 420 is the lowest common denominator for 3, 4, 5, and 7. You work this out as follows: 3 x 4 x 5 x 7 = 420.

Week 3: Three students got a grade A. To work this out, first find the common denominator for the numbers 3, 4, 6, and 8. The only common denominator less than 30 is 24. Therefore, 8 students got a grade B, 6 a grade B–, 4 a grade C and 3 of them failed. This represents 21 of the students; which means that the remaining 3 were awarded a grade A.

Week 4: If Mike eats 3 times as fast as Luke, he must be able to eat 3 times as many dumplings as his brother. Therefore, Mike eats 24 while Luke eats 8 (32 ÷ 4 = 8). Together it takes them 45 minutes.

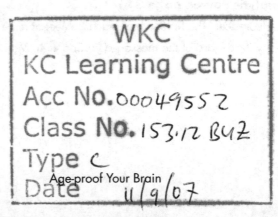
Age-proof Your Brain

Index